quick crochet
huge hooks

quick crochet
huge hooks

SALLY HARDING

**photography by
John Heseltine**

MITCHELL BEAZLEY

Quick Crochet Huge Hooks

First published in 2005 by Mitchell Beazley,
an imprint of Octopus Publishing Group Ltd.,
2–4 Heron Quays, London E14 4JP

ISBN 1 84533 021 8

A CIP record of this book is available from the British Library

Senior Executive Editor Anna Sanderson
Executive Art Editor Auberon Hedgecoe
Project manager Susan Berry
Design Anne Wilson
Illustrations Kate Simunek
Production Seyhan Esen

Set in Myriad

Colour origination by Chroma Graphics, Singapore
Printed and bound in China by Toppan Printing Company Ltd.

contents

introduction...

In the middle of working on a book on giant-needle knitting, I couldn't resist the temptation to rush out and buy a huge crochet hook and see what kind of textures I could come up with. The results were even more exciting than I imagined they would be – really seductive fabrics with giant loops. And on top of this, I found it was amazingly quick, much faster than working with fat knitting needles. Since I am as passionate about crochet as I am about knitting – maybe even more so – producing a sister book on huge-hook crochet quickly became my next mission.

To entice absolute beginners into the craft and to provide inspiration for seasoned crocheters as well, I have filled the following pages with very simple projects made from a wide range of good-quality yarns, all worked on huge hooks. The inclusion of step-by-step instructions for all the basic crochet techniques means anyone can also use this book to learn crochet from scratch. Tips for adding fun trims – like pompoms, beads, fringe – are included, too.

My huge-hook crochet collection consists of scarves, bags, throws, a rug, and cushions. No complicated stitches have been used; in fact, the majority of projects are worked in simple double crochet – the easiest stitch to learn. Everything, with the exception of the String Shopper on page 54, is square, rectangular, or circular, so there's no complex shaping involved either.

Whenever I pick up a crochet hook and get going, I am reminded how enjoyable the actual process is, and working with great big hooks makes it even more so. To me, the versatility of crochet textures surpasses that of knitting – you can make just about any type of textile with crochet techniques, from fine intricate laces to draping wool scarves and sweaters or stiff string baskets. And it's so easy! Only one loop on the hook at a time also makes it hassle-free to stop and start, or to carry around wherever you go.

To give you a taster for the variety of crochet textures, I've included a range of yarn types – fine ones, superfat ones, rag strips, and string. Because the patterns are so easy – especially the scarves – I hope you'll use them as starters for your own original creations worked in any yarn you fancy. The beauty of huge-hook crochet is that the big loops show off the seductiveness of whatever threads you use and it's all finished in a flash. A scarf can be ready to wear in a few hours or a throw in a couple of days.

Like most crochet enthusiasts, I love introducing newcomers to this enjoyable craft and encouraging lapsed crocheters to look around and see all the exciting new yarns they can try. Huge-hook crochet will surely capture your imagination once you get started.

—Sally Harding

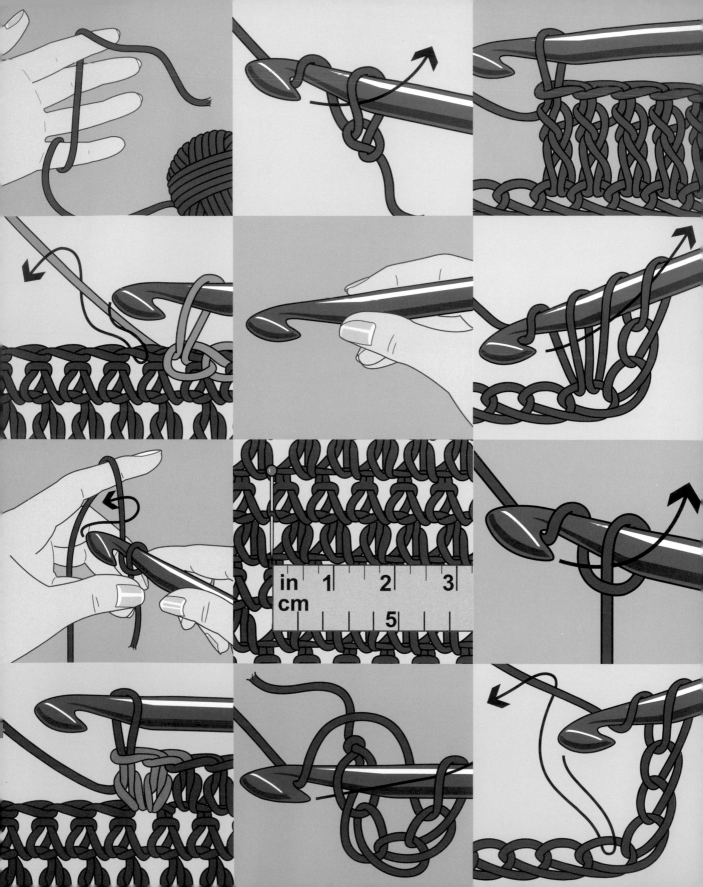

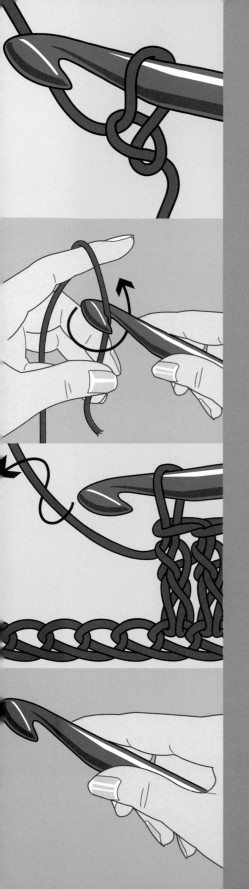

huge-hook
know-how

crochet basics...

There's no better way to learn to crochet than with a huge hook. The big loops are easy to see and quick to make. As a recent convert to huge-hook crochet, I would now always advise learners to avoid starting out with fine hooks – they make the craft look difficult to master, which it definitely is not. Begin with big, bold, beautiful loops and once you can crochet with ease, fine laces will be as easy as pie.

This chapter includes everything an absolute beginner needs to know to learn to crochet, from forming the first loop to working the tallest basic stitches. Crocheters who haven't crocheted for a number of years can use the instructions as a refresher course and for the huge-hook tips.

Before you get crocheting, read this page and the next and have a look at pages 12–15. They provide an introduction to yarns for huge hooks, explain what "huge" hooks are, and illustrate the scope and versatility of the resulting stunning textures.

yarns for huge hooks

The first sight of huge hooks usually makes one think of giant yarns and thick, unyielding textures. This couldn't be further from the truth. Superthick yarns can be worked with huge hooks, but so can fine and medium-weight yarns and strings and twines. How dense and stiff, or airy and flexible, the crochet fabric is depends on how thick the yarn is, how many strands are used together, and how huge the hook is. Any yarn can be used for huge-hook crochet. You can use it on its own as a single strand, or use several strands at once to thicken it, or twist it around other yarns to make your own version.

Crochet fabrics can also be formed with fabric strips. "Rag" crochet is ideal for bags and rugs, and I can't praise it enough. Making your own yarn from fabric remnants or old clothes opens up an exciting world of colour and texture.

To see just a few of the possibilities for unique huge-hook textures, turn to pages 12–15 for some life-size samples.

choosing huge hooks

My choice of what constitutes a "huge" hook is purely arbitrary. The range starts with a 10.00mm (US size N-13) hook and ends with a 20.00mm (US size S) – the hugest one I've been able to find. I decided to start the range with a 10.00mm (US size N-13) hook because until fairly recently it was the largest around and, though always intrigued by it, I was never quite sure what anyone did with it – at a time when superfat yarns were a rarity. Placed next to a standard-size hook, a 10.00mm (US size N-13) hook still looks truly huge.

Most of the designs in this book are worked with 12.00mm (US size O/P-15) and 15.00mm (US size Q) hooks, but lots are worked with a 10.00mm (US size N-13) – so you can start with these if you find holding a bigger hook awkward at first. Two designs, the Pompom Scarves on pages 50–53, are worked with the supergiant 20.00mm (US size S). If you decide you love using this giant, I leave it to you to try making scarves galore, or even throws, with it.

To find huge hooks, look in local stores or surf the net – see page 126 for my favourite sites. For a guide to comparative hook sizes, see page 127.

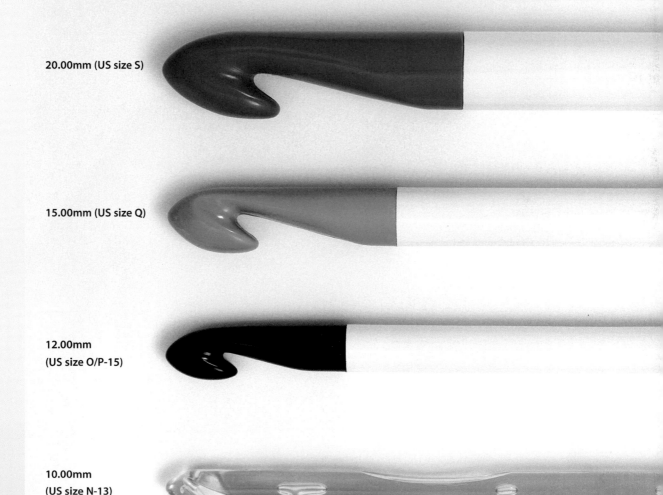

20.00mm (US size S)

15.00mm (US size Q)

**12.00mm
(US size O/P-15)**

**10.00mm
(US size N-13)**

huge-hook textures

The life-size crochet texture samples on these two pages and the two that follow show just a few of the many yarns you can use with huge hooks. All the swatches are worked in simple double crochet, each with a different hook size.

Included in the yarns are mohair, cotton, tape, superthick wool, chunky chenille, and fabric strips.

Crochet lends itself to anything malleable and other textures you could try out are leather, raffia, string, and wire.

Airy crochet textures are perfect for scarves and lightweight throws; medium-density ones make good cushion covers, warm throws, and floppy bags; while really dense crochet is ideal for stand-alone bags, baskets, and rugs.

Double crochet worked with a 10.00mm (US size N-13) crochet hook, a medium-weight cotton yarn, and a medium-weight mohair yarn.

Double crochet worked with a 12.00mm (US size O/P-15) crochet hook, cotton tape yarn, a chunky chenille yarn, and narrow silk fabric strips.

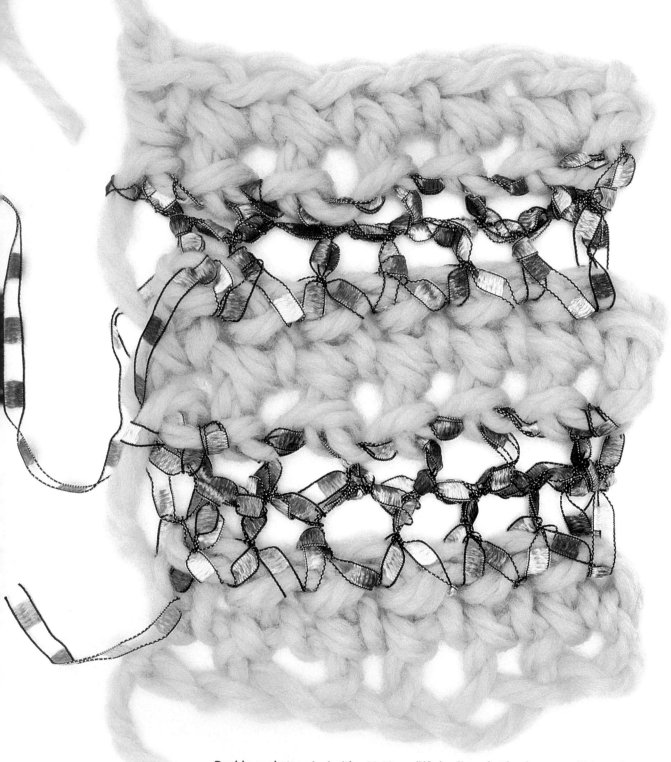

Double crochet worked with a 20.00mm (US size S) crochet hook, a superthick wool yarn, and a novelty tape yarn (see page 126 for where to obtain this unusual yarn).

Double crochet worked with a 15.00mm (US size Q) crochet hook and wide silk fabric strips.

learning to crochet...

The best way to pick up crochet techniques is to have someone sitting by your side showing you how it's done. But if you're not lucky enough to have a personal tutor, here are clear, simple instructions for teaching yourself the main crochet stitches.

If you're starting to learn crochet from scratch, purchase a 12.00mm (US size O/P-15) hook and some chunky wool or synthetic wool-type yarn. Wool yarns are easy to manipulate because they have just the right amount of elasticity to glide on and off the hook with ease. A 12.00mm (US size O/P-15) hook is nice and big but more manageable for a beginner than the two largest sizes.

All crochet starts with a simple sliding knot called a "slip knot". Before making this first loop, try various ways of holding your hook and yarn to familiarize yourself with these simple tools of the craft.

holding the yarn

In crochet, the yarn is held in the left hand and the hook in the right (left-handers will have to reverse everything, using a mirror for the illustrations). There are any number of ways to lace the yarn around the fingers of the left hand and the lacing shown here (see right) is a popular method. Try this lacing, then gently pull the tail end of the yarn. The aim is for the fingers to hold the yarn with a bit of tension, allowing it to slide freely over the tip of the forefinger as more yarn is needed to create the stitches. If you first learned to crochet with a different lacing technique, stick to it, because you will probably have better control with the method you learned first. For instance, many crocheters feed the yarn over the tip of the middle finger rather than the forefinger, grasping the crochet between the forefinger and thumb rather than between the middle finger and thumb.

holding the hook

The knife position (see below) is probably the best way to hold a huge hook if you are an absolute beginner, because it puts less pressure on the wrist. But try the "pencil" position, too, when learning how to make chain stitches (see page 18) just in case it suits you better.

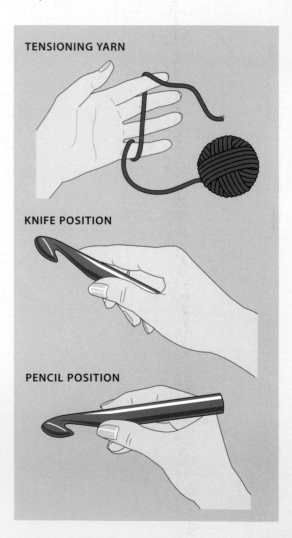

TENSIONING YARN

KNIFE POSITION

PENCIL POSITION

making the first loop

1 Position the yarn and hook as explained on the previous page, then pinch the tail end of the yarn between the thumb and middle finger of the left hand. Grab the yarn with the hook and twirl the tip around the yarn in the direction shown by the arrow to form a loop on the hook.

2 To prevent the new loop on the hook from closing up too tightly, grip the bottom of it and the tail end of the yarn between the left thumb and middle finger. Move the hook around the yarn as shown by the arrow to form a "wrap" around the hook.

3 Now draw the "wrap" on the hook through the loop as shown by the arrow (A). This creates a slip knot on the hook (B). Pull both ends of the yarn to tighten the knot under the hook, but keep it loose enough to allow the loop to expand freely.

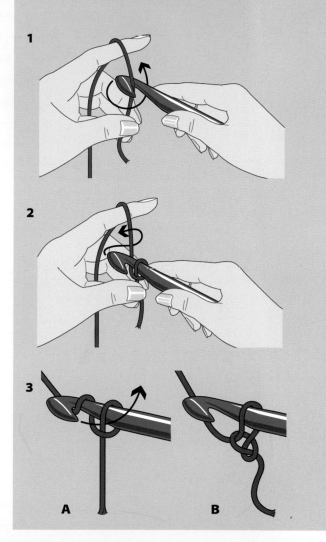

basic stitch symbols

Crochet patterns are often given in symbols. Even if you are an absolute beginner, it's a good idea to learn the symbols for the main crochet stitches right away. They show clearly how the stitches relate to each other sizewise and how they fit together in rows (see page 21). The crochet symbols here are a commonly used set. Different countries use slightly different symbols – all are easy to learn and bear a resemblance to the stitches they represent.

☻	= first foundation
◯	= chain (ch)
⌢	= slip stitch (ss)
✚	= double crochet (dc)
⊤	= half treble crochet (htr)
⊤	= treble crochet (tr)
⊤	= double treble (dtr)

preparing the foundation...

To start a piece of crochet, you create a base on which to work the first row of stitches. For a simple rectangular piece of crochet, this base consists of a length of chain stitches called a "foundation chain".

Easy crochet stitches to learn, chain stitches are also used at the beginning of rows as part of the selvedge and in combination with other stitches to form all kinds of crochet textures and laces.

If you are a novice, before trying to make your first chain stitches, practise making slip knots (see page 17) until you can make one without looking at the illustrations. Mastering your first loop will teach you good yarn and hook control and give you the confidence to proceed, so don't rush it. Each repetition will improve your dexterity.

making a foundation chain

Crochet instructions start by telling you how many chains to make as the foundation for your first row of stitches. If 30 foundation chains are required, the instructions say "30ch". Making a chain stitch is as easy as it looks, but it takes a little practice until you can make them with just the right degree of tightness. Beginners should err on the side of loops that are a bit too loose, rather than too tight. With a little practice your fingers will find the right movements to make perfectly formed, even chains.

1 Make a slip knot, then grab the yarn with the hook as shown by the arrow (at the same time you can swivel the left hand slightly so you are wrapping the yarn with the left hand and grabbing with the hook simultaneously to speed up the movement).

2 Holding the slip knot between the middle finger and the thumb of the left hand, pull the yarn wrapped around the hook through the loop on the

hook to complete your first chain stitch. These first two steps are called in crochet terminology "yrh (yarn round hook) and draw a lp (loop) through".

3 Make as many chains as required. Always count the stitches in your completed foundation chain to double check, but don't count the loop on the hook.

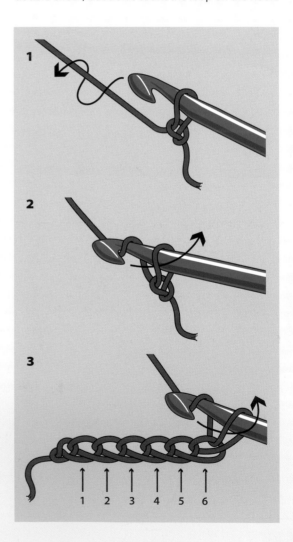

learning double crochet...

The first crochet stitch a beginner should learn is double crochet. It can be worked in combination with other crochet stitches to form texture patterns or on its own to create a crochet textile called "double crochet". Because of its ease of execution, double crochet has been used for many of the projects in this book. Beginners will love how easy it is to master.

The most versatile of all crochet stitches, double crochet can be worked tightly for firm textiles or loosely for airy ones. All the swatches on pages 12–15 have been worked back and forth in rows of double crochet. A smoother surface is achieved when the stitches are worked in the round, as on the bags on pages 60–67.

working double crochet

The steps on this page explain how to make double crochet stitches on a foundation chain. All individual double crochet stitches are made in the same way – the only variation is what you work them into. The first row is worked into a chain and the following rows are worked into the stitches of the previous row. Practise working double crochet into a chain as here until you get the hang of it, then turn to page 22 for how to work the following rows.

1 Make a foundation chain of about 12 chains. Holding the chains with the left hand, insert the hook from front to back through the *second* chain from the hook, wrap the yarn round the hook as shown by the arrow, and draw a loop of the yarn through the chain – there are now two loops on the hook. (You can insert the hook under one or two strands of the chain, but inserting it under one, as here, is easier for a beginner – see page 31 for a variation.)

2 Next, wrap the yarn round the hook ("yrh") and draw it through the two loops on the hook. This completes the first double crochet – called "dc". In a crochet pattern, what you have just done is called "1dc in 2nd ch from hook".

3 Work one double crochet in each of the remaining chains in the same way to complete the first row.

learning treble crochet...

After double crochet, the two most frequently used crochet stitches are half treble crochet and treble crochet. Like double crochet stitches, each of these can be used in combination with other stitches for a variety of crochet textures or on their own. Half trebles are slightly taller than double crochet and trebles are slightly taller than half trebles (see symbols on pages 17 and 22). Treble crochet stitches used on their own create a more airy, less firm textile than double crochet or half treble crochet, which makes it more pliable and softer.

Try both these stitches with the same yarn and hook that you used to make a swatch of double crochet to see how the stitches compare.

working half trebles

Make sure you have completely mastered double crochet before trying half trebles. The method of working is similar, so if you can work double crochet effortlessly, learning half trebles will be a cinch. Follow these steps to work your first row, then turn to page 22 to learn how to work the following rows.

1 First, make a foundation chain of about 13 chains. Wrap the yarn round the hook ("yrh"), simultaneously grabbing the yarn with the hook and moving the yarn forwards slightly with the left hand to facilitate the movement. Then with the "wrap" in place, insert the hook from front to back through the *third* chain from the hook (under one or two strands of the chain), work a "yrh" as shown by the arrow, and draw a loop through the chain – there are now three loops on the hook.

2 Next, work a "yrh" and draw it through all three loops on the hook as shown by the arrow. This completes the first half treble – called "htr".

In a crochet pattern, what you have just done is called "1htr in 3rd ch from hook".

3 Work one half treble in each of the remaining chains in the same way to complete the first row of half treble crochet.

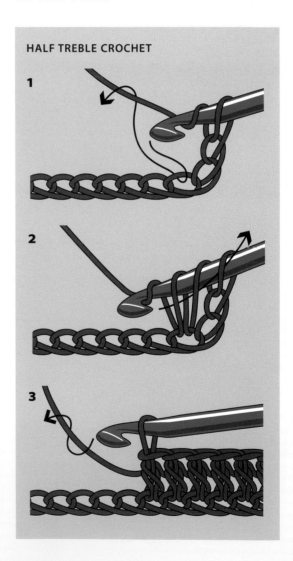

HALF TREBLE CROCHET

1

2

3

working trebles

Follow the steps on this page to work the first row of the simple treble crochet textile. Then turn to page 22 to learn how to work more rows.

Practise making trebles before you try making the taller crochet stitches explained on page 23. The technique for making these taller stitches – called double, triple, quadruple, and quintuple trebles – is almost exactly the same, except that they are started with more wraps on the hook.

1 Make a foundation chain of about 14 chains. Wrap the yarn round the hook ("yrh"). Then insert the hook from front to back through the *fourth* chain from the hook, work a "yrh" as shown by the arrow, and draw a loop through the chain – there are now three loops on the hook.

2 Next, work a "yrh" and draw it through the first two loops on the hook as shown by the arrow – two loops now remain on the hook.

3 Work a "yrh" and draw it through the two loops on the hook as shown by the arrow. This completes the first treble – called "tr". In a crochet pattern, what you have just done is called "1tr in 4th ch from hook".

4 Work one treble in each of the remaining chains in the same way to complete the first row of treble crochet.

TREBLE CROCHET

1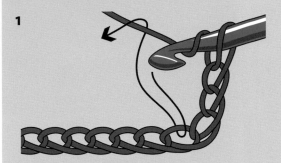

2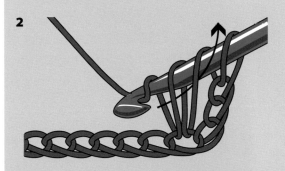

3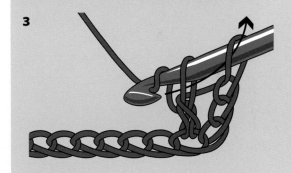

4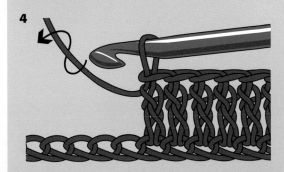

how to turn for next row...

rows in symbols

This is where crochet symbols prove their worth. A few rows of doubles, half trebles, and trebles shown in symbols give an understanding at a glance of how many chain stitches you'll need at the beginning of a row (called "turning chain"). They also show how the three chains at the beginning of a row of treble crochet are a substitute for the first treble (and are counted as "one" stitch). See page 17 for the symbol key.

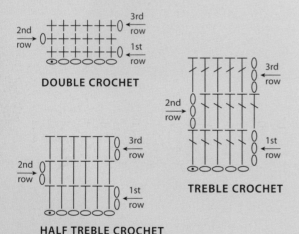

The first row of a rectangular piece of crochet is worked into a length of chain stitches as explained on pages 18 through 21. On the following rows the stitches are worked into the stitches of the previous row.

After completing the first row, turn the crochet so the other side of the stitches are facing you and the hook and the loop on it are at the right-hand edge. Crochet instructions will always remind you at the end of a row to "turn" the work. In order to bring the yarn up to the height of the stitch you are working, you work one or more chain stitches at the edge of the crochet before working into the top of the row below. If working double crochet, make one chain; for half treble crochet, work two chains; and for treble crochet, work three chains (see below).

To complete the second row of double crochet or of half treble crochet, work one stitch into each stitch in the row below, inserting the hook under both strands of the chain-shaped loop at the top of the stitch (see arrow). To complete the second row of treble crochet, miss the first stitch below and work one stitch into the top of the second stitch (see arrow), then work one stitch into each of the remaining stitches. Work the last treble crochet in the third of the three chains at the edge (see symbols left). Work all the following rows in the same way.

DOUBLE CROCHET

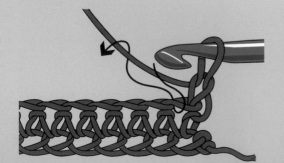

HALF TREBLE CROCHET

TREBLE CROCHET

more stitches...

There are only two more basic stitches to learn in order to follow any possible crochet pattern – slip stitches and double trebles. A slip stitch is the shortest crochet stitch, and a double treble is the first of a series of the tallest crochet stitches.

working slip stitches

Rows of slip stitches are rarely used to form a crochet fabric, but a single row of slip stitches in a contrasting colour can be used to create a neat, simple edging (see V-stitch Bag on page 67). More commonly, a single slip stitch is used as a connecting stitch to join a foundation chain into a ring or to join the yarn to a new position on the crochet fabric.

Slip stitches along a row

To work slip stitches along a row (see top right), insert the hook into the next stitch and wrap the yarn round the hook as shown by the arrow, then draw the yarn through the stitch and the loop on the hook in one movement – called "1ss".

Joining with a slip stitch

Individual slip stitches are used in many patterns in this book to join a foundation ring, the base for a piece of circular crochet. First make as many chain stitches as instructed, then insert the hook through the first chain and draw a loop through the chain and the loop on the hook (see centre right). This is called "join with a ss in first ch to form a ring".

working taller stitches

Double trebles are worked in almost exactly the same way as trebles except that each stitch is started with two wraps on the hook instead of one and the hook is inserted into the *fifth* chain from the hook in the foundation chain. All the loops are then

SLIP STITCHES ALONG A ROW

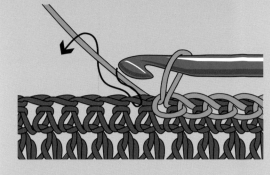

JOINING WITH A SLIP STITCH

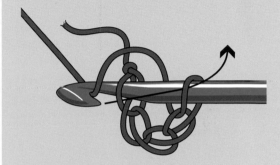

WORKING A DOUBLE TREBLE

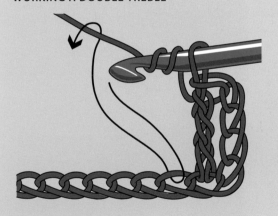

worked off two at a time, as for trebles. The second and following rows of double trebles are worked as for trebles, except four chains (instead of three) are worked at the start of the row for "turning" chains.

Taller trebles – triple trebles, quadruple trebles, and quintuple trebles – are begun with three, four, or five wraps on the hook, and are worked using the same principle as trebles. Your pattern will state how many "turning" chains to use for these stitches.

increasing and decreasing...

Adding more stitches to a row of crochet is a technique called "increasing". Reducing the number of stitches is called "decreasing". Adding stitches on a piece of straight crochet widens the fabric and subtracting stitches narrows it, so these simple techniques are used for shaping your crochet.

Adding stitches in crochet is much simpler than in knitting, because it is so easy to work two or more stitches into the same spot. Subtracting from the number of stitches is just as easy – you can either miss stitches in the row below or half-finish two or more stitches (leaving the last loop of each stitch on the hook) and then join them by drawing a single loop through all the stitches. Your crochet pattern will tell you exactly how to work increases and decreases, but have a look at these very simple ones to understand the principle of the techniques.

working a simple increase

To add one stitch in a row of double crochet, just work two double crochet into the same stitch in the row below (see below left). This is called "2dc in next dc".

working a simple decrease

To decrease one stitch in a row of double crochet, draw a loop through each of the next two stitches, then draw a loop through all three loops on the hook as shown by the arrow (see bottom left). In a crochet pattern this is called "[insert hook in next dc, yrh and draw a lp through] twice, yrh and draw through all 3 lps on hook".

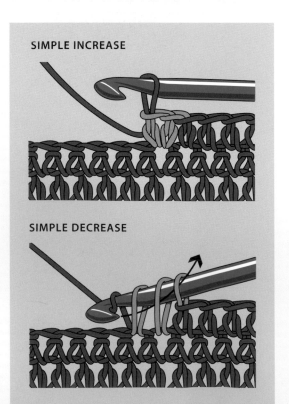

SIMPLE INCREASE

SIMPLE DECREASE

fastening off

When your piece of crochet is finished there will still be one loop on the hook. Securing this last loop so that your crochet does not unravel is called "fastening off". To fasten off, first cut the yarn – called "break off" – leaving a tail of yarn at least 15cm/6in long. Then draw the yarn end through the loop, and pull tight (see below).

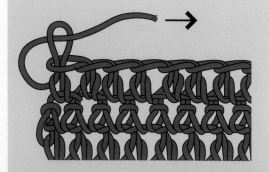

following a crochet pattern...

The step-by-step instructions on the previous pages are a sound preparation for following any crochet pattern. They include an introduction to crochet terminology and abbreviations and how to work all the basic stitches found in crochet patterns. Special stitch patterns that are a combination of or a manipulation of basic stitches are always explained fully within a pattern.

Crochet patterns are generally all laid out in a similar way. They start by giving the size of the finished item. Following this is a list of yarn, hooks, and any other materials you'll need. Next comes the recommended tension (see right) and any special tips you need to read before starting.

crochet abbreviations

Abbreviations in the row-by-row instructions of a crochet pattern make the patterns shorter, and easier and quicker to follow. Crochet terminology and abbreviations may seem confusing at first glance, but you will quickly realize that they make the patterns crystal clear; they are logical and really easy to learn. For example, "1dc in next st" means work one double crochet stitch in the next stitch in the row below. For easy reference, all the crochet abbreviations used in this book are given at the back (see page 127).

tip boxes in the patterns

Tip boxes and special how-to boxes are sprinkled throughout the instructions for the huge-hook designs. Pay special attention to these and to the Before You Start sections at the beginning of the patterns – they are the tips an advanced crocheter would give you if they were letting you in on their years of experience.

tension

Everybody crochets with their own personal style. Several crocheters sitting side by side using the same size hook and yarn and working the same number of stitches will create pieces of crochet of a similar size but not precisely the same. Because there is no right or wrong crochet tightness, there's no need to try to alter your own style. Every crochet pattern specifies what size of stitch you should aim to achieve – this is called the "tension". A tension tells you how many stitches and rows there should be over 10cm (4in) of crochet. Before you begin a crochet pattern you can test your tension by making a swatch of crochet and measuring the number of stitches and rows to 10cm (4in). If necessary, you can use a different hook size to increase or decrease the size of the stitches. However, if you are a beginner working with huge hooks, don't be too concerned about stitch size. Tension will become more important when you start crocheting fitted garments, but for now just have fun with huge loops. If in doubt, err on the side of forming slightly looser loops so your huge hook can glide easily in and out of the stitches.

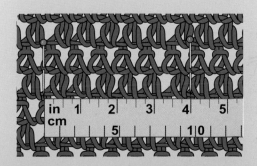

projects

three-row scarf

Warm and cosy, this narrow wool scarf is the quickest project in the book to work. It is crocheted with a huge hook that is 15 millimetres in diameter (US size Q) – the second largest hook on the market. Worked end to end, instead of side to side in the usual way, it is 62 stitches long but only three rows wide! Because it is made entirely in treble crochet, it is perfect for a beginner who wants to practise crocheting these simple, tall stitches. After speeding through the scarf, take your time to weave in and knot on the elegant fringe, using a superchunky variegated wool yarn in your chosen colour.

here's how...

The foundation-chain edge of this scarf looks better if each stitch in the first row is worked into the back loop of each chain. This makes the first row of this scarf slower, but the last two go quickly.

how big is it?
The finished scarf measures approximately 9cm/3¾in wide (width of centre section, not flared ends) x 140cm/54¼in long, excluding fringe.

which stitches?
Treble crochet (tr)

how much yarn?
MC = superchunky wool yarn in main colour
  1 x 100g/3½oz ball Rowan *Big Wool*
  (lime – shade no. 029 – or chosen colour)
CC = superchunky variegated wool yarn in contrasting colour
  small amount of Rowan *Biggy Print*
  (variegated mauve and cherry – shade no.
  246 – or chosen colour)
(*See page 124 for yarn tips*)

which hooks?
15.00mm and 20.00mm (US sizes Q and S) crochet hooks

or make this!

With one ball of Rowan *Big Wool* for the main colour you can make a longer scarf – 169cm/65in long – if you like. Just make 77 chains to start, for a scarf with 75 stitches.

what tension?
4 sts and 3 rows to 9cm/3½in measured over tr using MC and 15.00mm (US size Q) hook.

before you start
- There is no need to check your tension before beginning, as an exact scarf size is not essential.
- If you don't have a 20.00mm (US size S) crochet hook for working the foundation chain, use the 15.00mm (US size Q) and work very loosely.
- *For crochet abbreviations, turn to page 127.*

make the foundation chain
The scarf is worked from end to end instead of from side to side in the usual way. Using a 20.00mm (US size S) hook and MC, make 64ch.
Change to 15.00mm (US size Q) hook.
1st row 1tr in 4th ch from hook, 1tr in each of rem 60ch. Turn.
2nd row 3ch (to count as first tr), miss first tr and work 1tr in next tr, 1tr in each of rem tr, ending with 1tr in 3rd of 3ch. Turn. (62 sts)
3rd row As for 2nd row.
Fasten off by cutting yarn, passing yarn end through loop on hook, and pulling tight.

finishing touches
Before beginning fringe, weave in any loose ends.
Fringe
For each end of scarf make fringe as foll:
Cut five strands of CC each 95cm/37½in long.
Using your fingers, weave one strand of CC in and out of first 6 sts of first row of tr; then weave same strand back through same sts but *over* sts the first weaving went *under* and *under* sts the first weaving went *over*. Adjust these two fringe strands so they are equal lengths. Weave strands through other two

rows in same way. Weave rem two strands through gaps at tops of first 8 sts of first and second rows (at base of sts of row above). Knot tog two ends of each woven strand close to edge of scarf to secure. Then knot each length of fringe at end (about 19cm/7¹/₂in from edge of scarf) and trim off yarn 6mm/¹/₄in from knot.

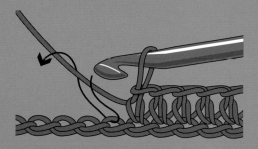

make a chain edge like this!

For a professional finish, you can make the foundation-chain edge of your crochet match the edge along the final row of crochet. To do this, work each stitch in the first row of stitches into the back loop of each chain as shown by the arrow above. This leaves a neat edge of linked chain stitches along the edge that exactly matches the linked chain along the top of the final row of crochet stitches. It can be hard to identify the back loop of the foundation chain on big loops, so you might want to practise this first with a 10.00mm (US size N-13) hook before starting your scarf.

alternative scarf

For an alternative, work the scarf with only two rows, then work double crochet in a contrasting colour evenly around the edge, with three stitches in each corner.

striped mohair scarf

The lofty, airy lightness of this narrow scarf (left) is achieved quite simply – by working medium-weight and lightweight yarns with a huge hook. Though the predominant feel of the scarf is of a soft mohair, it also contains the contrasting textures of chunky chenille and a cotton and silk blend yarn. A linen tape yarn, woven along the length of the stitches as a finishing touch, sparks off these subtle stripes. Because each row of the scarf is worked end to end instead of from side to side in the usual way, the yarn ends form a self-fringe. Instructions for working a wider version of the scarf (see right) are given in the tip box on page 35.

here's how...

The instructions here are for the narrow scarf on page 32. If you want to make the wider scarf on page 33, see the tip box opposite.

how big is it?
The finished scarf measures approximately 9.5cm/3³⁄₄in wide x 130cm/52in long, excluding fringe.

which stitches?
Double crochet (dc)

how much yarn?
A = chunky chenille yarn in first colour
  1 x 100g/3¹⁄₂oz ball Rowan *Chunky Cotton Chenille* in chosen colour (aqua blue – shade no. 392 – or chosen colour)
B = medium-weight mohair yarn in second colour
  1 x 50g/1³⁄₄oz ball Rowan *Kid Classic*
(light blue – shade no. 818 – or chosen colour)
C = fine mohair yarn in third colour
  1 x 25g/1oz ball Rowan *Kid Silk Haze*
  (grape – shade no. 600 – or chosen colour)
D = lightweight silk and cotton yarn in fourth colour
  1 x 50g/1³⁄₄oz hank Rowan *Summer Tweed*
  (orange – shade no. 509 – or chosen colour)
E = viscose and linen tape yarn in fifth colour
  1 x 50g/1³⁄₄oz ball Rowan *Linen Print*
  (variegated pastels – shade no. 345 – or chosen colour)
(*See page 124 for yarn tips*)

which hook?
10.00mm (US size N-13) crochet hook

what tension?
8 sts and 11¹⁄₂ rows to 10cm/4in measured over dc stripe patt using 10.00mm (US size N-13) hook.

alternative colourways
You can use yarns left over from this project or others in the book to make more scarves in your own stripe sequences. The trick to a successful design is to keep your palette limited and to use a mixture of yarn textures as shown here. Before starting your scarf, crochet small striped swatches to try out your colour combinations and stripe widths.

before you start

- There is no need to check your tension before beginning, as an exact scarf size is not essential.
- To create a neat chain edge along the foundation-chain edge of the scarf, see page 31.
- Remember to work each row of the scarf with a new length of yarn, leaving a long loose end at the beginning and end of each row. These ends form the "self-fringe". Leave ends at least 15cm/6in long. If making the wider version (see right), leave 20cm/8in ends.
- *For crochet abbreviations, turn to page 127.*

make the foundation chain

The scarf is worked from end to end instead of from side to side in the usual way.

Using a 10.00mm (US size N-13) hook and one strand A and leaving a long loose end before first chain, make 104ch loosely.

Fasten off A, leaving a long loose end. (The long loose end at beg and end of each row will form fringe.)

1st row Using one strand A and leaving a long loose end, insert hook in first ch, yrh and draw a loop through—called *join yarn with a ss*—, 1ch, 1dc in same place as ss, 1dc in each of rem 103ch. Turn. (104dc)

Fasten off A, leaving a long loose end.

2nd row Using one strand B and leaving a long loose end, join yarn with a ss in first dc, 1ch, 1dc in same place as ss, 1dc in each of rem 103dc. Turn. Fasten off B, leaving a long loose end.

Cont in this way, starting every row with a new strand of yarn, leaving long loose ends at each end, and working in dc stripes as foll:

1 row more in B, using one strand.

2 rows C, using two strands of yarn held tog.

or make this!

For the wider version of the striped mohair scarf (shown on page 33), work the stripes as for the main scarf, then work eight more rows in stripes as follows:

2 rows C, using two strands.

1 row Rowan *Summer Tweed* in lilac (shade 501), using one strand.

2 rows C, using two strands held tog.

2 rows B, using one strand.

1 row A, using one strand. Fasten off.

Then weave two strands of Rowan *Linen Print* (shade 347) through the two stripes worked in *Summer Tweed*. Tie fringe at the ends as for the main scarf, but dividing strands into seven groups, and trimming to 10cm/4in.

1 row D, using one strand.

2 rows C, using two strands of yarn held tog.

2 rows B, using one strand.

1 row A, using one strand.

Fasten off.

finishing touches

Using a yarn needle and two strands E, weave yarn from end to end of scarf through sts of row worked with yarn D, leaving long loose ends in fringe.

Fringe

At each end of scarf, divide fringe strands into four groups of strands and knot each group tog close to scarf edge. Then trim fringe to 7.5cm/3in long.

loopy scarf

This loopy scarf is so much fun to make that you're sure to want to make it in different colours for different outfits, or as gifts for friends and family. The big loops are merely strands of yarn extended out from the simple double crochet stitches that are worked back and forth in short rows. They are quick to work and you'll pick up the technique in no time at all. Crocheted in superthick wool yarn, the scarf makes a snug winter warmer. I am dying to try it out in various types of novelty yarns – a fur one would be fun – or in mixtures of smooth and knobbly yarns. You can make the scarf as long as you like by just adding more rows.

here's how...

The narrow loopy scarf (see opposite page) is just one stitch narrower than the wide version (see page 37). Before you decide which width to make, work about six rows of each to see which one you like best. It's a good way to practise the loop stitch as well. Don't waste your yarn though: unravel the samples and reuse the yarn in the final scarf.

how big is it?
Wide loopy scarf: The finished scarf measures approximately 9cm/3¹/₂in wide x 138cm/55in long.
Narrow loopy scarf: The finished scarf measures approximately 7.5cm/3in wide x 146cm/58in long.

which stitches?
Double-crochet loop stitch

how much yarn?
Wide loopy scarf
MC = superchunky bicolour wool yarn in main colour
  2 x 100g/3¹/₂oz balls Rowan *Big Wool*
  (black and grey – shade no. 11 – or chosen colour)
CC = superchunky bicolour wool yarn in contrasting colour
  1 x 100g/3¹/₂oz ball Rowan *Big Wool*
  (off-white and grey – shade no. 13 – or chosen colour)
Narrow loopy scarf
MC = superchunky bicolour wool yarn in main colour
  1 x 100g/3¹/₂oz ball Rowan *Big Wool*
  (black and grey – shade no. 11 – or chosen colour)
CC = superchunky bicolour wool yarn in contrasting colour
  2 x 100g/3¹/₂oz balls Rowan *Big Wool*
  (off-white and grey – shade no. 13 – or chosen colour)
(*See page 124 for yarn tips*)

which hook?
12.00mm (US size O/P-15) crochet hook

what tension?
Approximately 6¹/₂ sts and 5¹/₂ rows to 10cm/4in measured over loop patt using 12.00mm (US size O/P-15) hook.

before you start
- There is no need to check your tension before beginning the project, as an exact scarf size is not essential.
- *For crochet abbreviations, turn to page 127.*

wide loopy scarf

make the foundation chain
The Wide Loopy Scarf (see page 37) is made up of two identical pieces that are joined tog end to end.
First piece
Using a 12.00mm (US size O/P-15) hook and CC, make 7ch.
1st patt row Insert hook in 2nd ch from hook, then with yarn around index finger as usual pick up yarn behind finger instead of in front of it and draw a loop through while keeping a 6.5cm/2¹/₂in long loop around forefinger, drop loop off finger (but keep loop extended at back of work), yrh and draw a loop through both loops on hook to complete dc in usual way—called *loop-dc* or *lp-dc*—, work 1lp-dc in each of rem ch. Turn. (6 sts)
2nd patt row 1ch, work 1lp-dc in each lp-dc. Turn.
Rep last row 4 times more. (There are now 3 loop rows on each side of piece.) Break off CC.
Using MC, rep 2nd patt row until piece measures 69cm/27¹/₂in from foundation-ch edge –

approximately 32 rows MC (16 loop rows on each side of piece). Fasten off.

Second piece

Make in exactly same way as first piece.

finishing touches

Aligning two pieces of scarf, stitch tog along edges of last row. Weave in any loose ends.

narrow loopy scarf

make the foundation chain

The Narrow Loopy Scarf (see above right) is made up of two identical pieces that are joined tog end to end.

First piece

Using a 12.00mm (US size O/P-15) hook and CC, make 6ch.

1st patt row Work as for 1st patt row of Wide Loopy Scarf. Turn. (5 sts)

2nd patt row Work as for 2nd patt row of Wide Loopy Scarf.

Rep last row 4 times more. (There are now 3 loop rows on each side of piece.) Break off CC.

Rep 2nd patt row to form patt **and at the same time** work in stripes as foll:

[6 rows MC, 6 rows CC] twice.

6 rows MC.

4 rows CC.

Fasten off.

Second piece

Make in exactly same way as first piece.

finishing touches

Aligning two pieces of scarf, stitch tog along edges of last row. Weave in any loose ends.

narrow loopy scarf colourways

The Narrow Loopy Scarf (see above) is worked in the same colours as the wide version. For an alternative colourway (see below), work the pattern with the following stripe sequence: 6 rows of white and grey *Big Wool*, 4 rows of a variegated superthick yarn, [8 rows *Big Wool*, 4 rows variegated yarn] twice, 6 rows *Big Wool*.

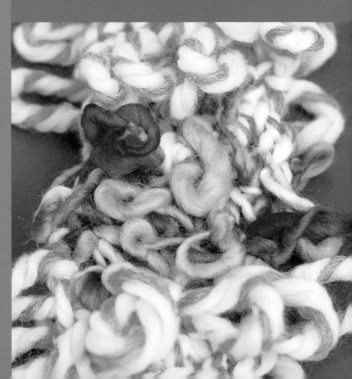

medallion scarves

If you are new to crochet, you will enjoy working traditional afghan medallions – they have a timeless appeal. If you make them for a scarf, rather than the usual blanket, you can finish the project in a fraction of the time. There are three medallions to choose from. Beginners can start with the Crosses Scarf (see right). Each of the medallions for this scarf is worked in just two quick rounds to make a stylish narrow scarf. The squares for the Diamonds Scarf on page 43 are worked in three rounds, and those for the Circles Scarf (see left) in four rounds. Using a cotton yarn gives a contemporary feel to this traditional design.

here's how...

There are three scarves to choose from. The Crosses scarf shown on page 41 uses the smallest medallion; the Diamonds scarf on the opposite page uses the medium-size medallion; and the Circles Scarf on page 40 uses the largest medallion.

how big is it?

Crosses scarf: When hanging, the finished scarf measures approximately 8.5cm/3¼in wide x 216cm/85in long.

Diamonds scarf: When hanging, the finished scarf measures approximately 9.5cm/3¾in wide x 155cm/61in long.

Circles scarf: When hanging, the finished scarf measures approximately 14cm/5½in wide x 159cm/62½in long.

(*For size of medallions, see What Tension? on page 44*)

which stitches?

Crosses scarf
- Treble crochet (tr)

Diamonds scarf
- Treble crochet (tr)
- Double crochet (dc)

or make this!

The square medallions used for these scarves are usually used to make afghans, so you can turn this pattern into a lightweight throw by working lots more of them. For a winter warmer, make the motifs using a 15.00mm (US size Q) hook and a superthick yarn such as Rowan *Big Wool*.

- Half treble crochet (htr)

Circles scarf
- Treble crochet (tr)
- Double treble crochet (dtr)
- Half treble crochet (htr)
- Double crochet (dc)

how much yarn?

Crosses scarf

A = lightweight silk and cotton blend yarn in first contrasting colour

  1 x 50g/1¾oz hank Rowan *Summer Tweed*
  (off-white – shade no. 524 – or chosen colour)

B = medium-weight cotton yarn in second contrasting colour

  2 x 50g/1¾oz balls Rowan *All Seasons Cotton*
  (deep navy – shade no. 164 – or chosen colour)

Diamonds scarf

A = lightweight silk and cotton blend yarn in first contrasting colour

  1 x 50g/1¾oz hank Rowan *Summer Tweed*
  (lime – shade no. 527 – or chosen colour)

B = lightweight silk and cotton blend yarn in second contrasting colour

  1 x 50g/1¾oz hank Rowan *Summer Tweed*
  (turquoise – shade no. 512 – or chosen colour)

C = medium-weight cotton yarn in third contrasting colour

  2 x 50g/1¾oz balls Rowan *All Seasons Cotton*
  (deep navy – shade no. 164 – or chosen colour)

Circles scarf

A = lightweight silk and cotton blend yarn in first contrasting colour

  1 x 50g/1¾oz hank Rowan *Summer Tweed*
  (lime – shade no. 527 – or chosen colour)

B = lightweight silk and cotton blend yarn in second contrasting colour

1 x 50g/1³/₄oz hank Rowan *Summer Tweed*
(turquoise – shade no. 512 – or chosen colour)
C = medium-weight cotton yarn in third
contrasting colour
2 x 50g/1³/₄oz balls Rowan *All Seasons Cotton*
(deep navy – shade no. 164 – or chosen colour)
D = medium-weight cotton yarn in fourth
contrasting colour
1 x 50g/1³/₄oz ball Rowan *All Seasons Cotton*
(pale lime – shade no. 197 – or chosen colour)
(*See page 124 for yarn tips*)

which hook?

10.00mm (US size N-13) crochet hook

what tension?

Crosses scarf

Each medallion measures 9.5cm/3³/₄in square using
10.00mm (US size N-13) hook.

Diamonds scarf

Each medallion measures 11.5cm/4¹/₂in square using
10.00mm (US size N-13) hook.

Circles scarf

Each medallion measures 18cm/7in square using
10.00mm (US size N-13) hook.

before you start

- There is no need to check your tension before
  beginning, as an exact size is not essential for
  a scarf.
- To avoid having to weave in a loose end at centre
  of each medallion when finishing the scarf, work
  over the loose end when working the first round.
  To do this, wrap the strand of yarn clockwise in a
  circle behind the foundation-chain ring before
  beginning the first round. Then work the stitches
  of the first round over it.
- When fastening off the crochet at the end of a
  motif, leave a long loose end to use to sew the
  motifs together.
- *For crochet abbreviations, turn to page 127.*

crosses scarf

make the foundation ring

Using a 10.00mm (US size N-13) hook and A, make
3ch and join with a ss in first ch to form a ring.
1st rnd (RS) Using A, 3ch to count as first tr, 2tr in
ring, *2ch, 3tr in ring; rep from * twice more, 2ch,
break off A and using B join with a ss in 3rd of 3ch.
(Do not turn at end of rnds, but work with RS
always facing.)
2nd rnd Using B, 3ch, 1tr in each of next 2tr, *[2tr,
4ch, 2tr] all in next 2-ch sp, 1tr in each of next 3tr; rep
from * twice more, [2tr, 4ch, 2tr] all in next 2-ch sp,
join with a ss in 3rd of 3ch.
Fasten off.
Make 16 more medallions in same way.

finishing touches

Sew medallions together in a row. Knot rem loose
ends together in pairs and weave into work.

diamonds scarf

make the foundation ring

Using a 10.00mm (US size N-13) hook and A, make
3ch and join with a ss in first ch to form a ring.
1st rnd (RS) Using A, 3ch to count as first tr, 15tr in
ring, break off A and using B join with a ss in 3rd of
3ch. (Do not turn at end of rnds, but work with RS
always facing.)
2nd rnd Using B, 1ch, 1dc in same place as ss, *miss
1tr, 5htr in next tr, miss next tr, 1dc in next tr; rep
from * 3 times more omitting dc at end of last rep,
join with a ss in first dc. Fasten off B.
3rd rnd Using C, join with ss in centre htr of any 5htr-
group, 1ch, 1dc in same place as ss, *7tr in next dc
(after missing rem 2htr of 5htr-group), 1dc in centre
htr of next 5htr group; rep from * 3 times more
omitting 1dc at end of last rep, join with a ss in first dc.
Fasten off.

Make five more medallions in same way. Then make five medallions exactly the same, but using B for foundation ring and 1st rnd, and A for 2nd rnd.

finishing touches

Sew medallions together in a row, alternating two colourways. Weave in ends as for Crosses Scarf.

circles scarf

make the foundation ring

Using a 10.00mm (US size N-13) hook and A, make 4ch and join with a ss in first ch to form a ring.

1st rnd (RS) Using A, 3ch to count as first tr, 15tr in ring, break off A and using B join with a ss in 3rd of 3ch. (Do not turn at end of rnds, but work with RS always facing.)

2nd rnd Using B, 5ch, *1tr in next tr, 2ch; rep from * to end of rnd, break off B and using C join with a ss in 3rd of 5ch.

3rd rnd Using C, 6ch, 1dtr in same place as ss, *2ch, 1tr in next tr, 2ch, 1htr in next tr, 2ch, 1tr in next tr, 2ch, [1dtr, 2ch, 1dtr] all in next tr; rep from * twice more, 2ch, 1tr in next tr, 2ch, 1htr in next tr, 2ch, 1tr in next tr, 2ch, join with a ss in 4th of 6ch.

4th rnd Using C, 3dc in first 2-ch sp, *1dc in next dtr, 2dc in next sp, 1dc in next tr, 2dc in next sp, 1dc in next htr, 2dc in next sp, 1dc in next tr, 2dc in next sp, 1dc in next dtr, 3dc in next sp; rep from * twice more, 1dc in next dtr, 2dc in next sp, 1dc in next tr, 2dc in next sp, 1dc in next htr, 2dc in next sp, 1dc in next tr, 2dc in next sp, join with a ss in first dc. Fasten off.

Make three more medallions in same way. Then make four medallions exactly the same, but using D instead of A for foundation ring and 1st rnd.

finishing touches

Sew medallions together in a row, alternating two colourways. Weave in ends as for Crosses Scarf.

cross, diamond, and circle medallions
The cross medallion above has been enlarged to show the detail. For the size of this square and the diamond (see below) and circle (see bottom) medallions, see tension opposite.

cotton scarf
with beads

Worked in rows of simple double crochet using a soft cotton yarn, this bead-trimmed scarf is comfortable for fall, winter, and spring. Beads and huge-hook crochet are made for each other. Whether you're into small, subtle, delicate beads or big, bold, chunky ones, you can always find a huge-hook texture that will complement them perfectly. Rummaging through beads in a big bead store in central London is one of my favourite pastimes. There is usually some excuse to take me there, but I inevitably walk away with some extra beads that were not on my original list. Why not pick the beads for this scarf before you choose the yarn colours, so you can match the stripes to your delicious beads.

here's how...

If you want to make a neat chain along the foundation-chain edge of your scarf, work the first row of double crochet into the back loop of each chain (see page 31 for how to do this).

how big is it?
The finished scarf measures approximately 10.5cm/4$\frac{1}{4}$in wide x 160cm/64in long, excluding beaded fringe.

which stitches?
Double crochet (dc)

how much yarn?
MC = medium-weight cotton yarn in main colour
   2 x 50g/1$\frac{3}{4}$oz balls Rowan *All Seasons Cotton*
   (off-white – shade no. 178 – or chosen colour)
A = lightweight silk and cotton blend yarn in first contrasting colour
   small amount of Rowan *Summer Tweed*
   (raspberry – shade no. 528 – or chosen colour)
B = medium-weight cotton yarn in second contrasting colour
   small amount of Rowan *All Seasons Cotton*
   (coral – shade no. 183 – or chosen colour)
(*See page 124 for yarn tips*)

which hook?
10.00mm (US size N-13) crochet hook

what tension?
8 sts and 11 rows to 10cm/4in measured over dc stripes using 10.00mm (US size N-13) hook.

any extras?
10 flat round beads (coin-shaped), 12mm/$\frac{1}{2}$in in diameter, or beads of your choice

before you start
- There is no need to check your tension before beginning, as an exact size is not essential for a scarf.
- Instead of buying a whole ball of A and B, you can use your own yarn scraps for the contrasting stripes on this scarf. Or, if you do buy a whole ball each of A and B, you can make a second scarf to use up the leftovers, making A and B the main colours and MC the simple stripes.
- For a neat colour change between the stripes, change to the new colour with the last yrh of the previous row as instructed (see page 89).
- *For crochet abbreviations, turn to page 127.*

make the foundation chain
The scarf is worked from end to end instead of from side to side in the usual way.
Using a 10.00mm (US size N-13) hook and MC, make 129ch loosely.
1st row Using MC, 1dc in 2nd ch from hook, 1dc in each of rem 127ch. Turn. (128dc)
2nd row Using MC, 1ch, 1dc in each dc to last dc, insert hook in last dc, yrh and draw a loop through, break off MC and using A, yrh and draw through both loops on hook to complete last dc. Turn.
3rd row Using A, 1dc in each dc, breaking off A and changing to MC with last yrh of last dc. Turn.
Cont in dc, changing to a new colour with last yrh of last dc of previous row, and work in stripes as foll:
3 rows MC.
1 row B.
2 rows MC.
1 row A, changing to MC with last yrh of last dc.
Edging
Work next row and cont the edging around edge of scarf as foll:

Next rnd Using MC, 1dc in each dc to last dc, 3dc in last dc; then with same side still facing, work 6dc evenly along end of scarf and 3dc in corner; cont along long edge of scarf (foundation-ch edge) and work 1dc in each ch, then 3dc in next corner; work 6dc along other end of scarf, 2dc in corner and join with a ss in first dc of rnd.

finishing touches

Weave in any loose ends.

Twisted cords for fringe

Make five twisted cords for each end of scarf as foll: Cut five strands of MC, each 60cm/24in long, and make a 18cm/7in long twisted cord with each strand, knotting only one end of cords and leaving folded end unknotted (see page 123 for how to make twisted cords).

If your beads have small holes, attach knotted ends of five cords to each end of scarf, then attach beads (see caption right).

If your beads have a hole big enough for passing twisted cord through, pass folded end of first cord through centre of edge of scarf at one end, open loop at fold, pass cord through loop, and pull tight. Attach four other cords at equal intervals along end of scarf. Then cut off knot at end of first cord and, keeping twist pinched tog, pass it through bead. Reknot with bead approximately 9cm/3½in from edge of scarf. Secure a bead to each of rem cords in same way.

attaching small-holed beads

If your beads have only small holes, like the ones above, shown on an alternative colourway of the scarf, you can tie the beads to the ends of the twisted cords, using sewing thread that matches the beads.

pompom scarves

The pompoms add a little spark to these narrow chenille scarves worked with the very biggest crochet hook around – it's 20 millimetres in diameter (US size S). The giant hook creates a texture that looks like a complicated lace stitch, but it's really just rows of simple treble crochet worked with two strands of chunky chenille held together. Only three rows wide, the scarves are crocheted from end to end instead of from side to side in the usual way. They drape so beautifully that I am going to make several for myself in different colours and widths (not all with pompoms). Great to wear for a layered look.

here's how...

There are four lengths to choose from for these scarves. Before deciding how many chains to start with, find a scarf in your wardrobe that you like the length of and choose the length closest to this.

how big is it?
The finished scarves measure approximately 10.5cm/4^1/$_4$in wide and can be worked in four different lengths – 100[151.5:191.5:225.5]cm/ 40[60^1/$_2$:76^1/$_2$:90^1/$_4$]in, excluding the pompoms.

which stitches?
Treble crochet (tr)

how much yarn?
Green and blue scarves
MC = chunky cotton chenille yarn in main colour
   1[2: 2] x 100g/3^1/$_2$oz balls Rowan *Chunky Cotton Chenille* (light sage green – shade no. 393; or blue – shade no. 394)

Green scarf pompoms
A = chunky cotton chenille yarn in first contrasting colour
   small amount of Rowan *Chunky Cotton Chenille* (blue – shade no. 394 – or chosen colour)
B = lightweight silk and cotton blend yarn in second contrasting colour
   small amount of Rowan *Summer Tweed* (lime – shade no. 527 – or chosen colour)

Blue scarf pompoms
A = chunky cotton chenille yarn in first contrasting colour
   small amount of Rowan *Chunky Cotton Chenille* (light sage green – shade no. 393 – or chosen colour)
B = lightweight silk and cotton blend yarn in second contrasting colour

small amount of Rowan *Summer Tweed* (lime – shade no. 527 – or chosen colour)
(*See page 124 for yarn tips*)

which hook?
20.00mm (US size S) crochet hook

any extras?
* Strong cotton yarn that matches MC, for tying pompoms when making them
* Strong sewing thread that matches MC, for sewing on pompoms

what tension?
3^1/$_2$ sts and 3^1/$_2$ rows to 10cm/4in measured over tr using two strands MC and 20.00mm (US size S) hook.

before you start
* There is no need to check your tension before beginning, as an exact scarf size is not essential.
* To create a chain edge along the foundation-chain edge of the scarf, work the first row of tr into the back loop of each chain (see page 31).
* *For crochet abbreviations, turn to page 127.*

green scarf

make the foundation chain
The scarf is worked from end to end instead of from side to side in the usual way.
Using a 20.00mm (US size S) hook and two strands MC held tog, make 37[55:69:81]ch loosely.
1st row 1tr in 4th ch from hook, 1tr in each of rem 33[51:65:77]ch. Turn.
2nd row 3ch (to count as first tr), miss first tr and work 1tr in next tr, 1tr in each of rem tr, ending

with 1tr in 3rd of 3ch. Turn. (35[53:67:79] sts)
3rd row As 2nd row.
Fasten off.

finishing touches

Weave in any loose ends.
Pompoms
Make six pompoms in total – three for each end of
scarf – each 3.5cm/1³/₈in in diameter. Follow
instructions right, wrapping yarns A, B, and MC
around cardboard pompom-maker in that order.
Stitch three pompoms to each end of scarf with a
matching sewing thread.

blue scarf

make the foundation chain

Make the Blue Scarf exactly as for the Green Scarf.

finishing touches

Gather both ends of scarf with a single strand of MC.
Weave in any loose ends.
Dangling pompoms
Make six pompoms in total – three for each end of
scarf – each 3.5cm/1³/₈in in diameter. Follow
instructions right, wrapping yarns A, B, and MC
around cardboard pompom-maker in that order.
Then make six twisted cords in total – four 13cm/5in
long and two 16.5cm/6¹/₂in long (see page 123 for
how to make twisted cords). Leave folded ends of
twisted cords unknotted.
Using a matching sewing thread, stitch knotted end
of each cord to a pompom, hiding knot inside
pompom strands.
Join one long and two short dangling pompoms to
each end of scarf with a single strand of MC.

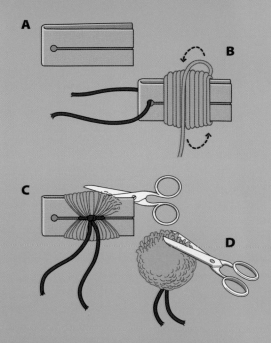

make quick pompoms!

You may have an excellent pompom-making
tool – and there are several types to choose
from – but if, like me, you find the one you have
slows the process down, try this technique. Cut
a 13–15cm/5–6in long strip of cardboard as
wide as the desired diameter of your pompom
(3.5cm/1³/₈in for the Pompom Scarves). Fold the
cardboard in half widthways and poke a hole
through the centre of both layers near the fold.
Then cut through the centre of the strip to the
holes as shown (A). Cut a length of strong yarn
for tying the pompom and thread it through
the holes. Next, wrap the yarn round and round
the cardboard until there's enough yarn for a
nice plump pompom (B). Slide the other end of
the tying strand through the cut slots and knot
tightly around the pompom. Cut through the
pompom yarn at the top and bottom, passing
the scissor blades between the layers (C). Slide
the pompom off the cardboard and trim the
shape to neatly round it (D).

string shopper

One of the best things about working with huge hooks is that you can form chunky stitches with string and twine. Made using green and olive garden twine and blue and turquoise packaging string, this sturdy crochet bag is perfect for casual weekend shopping. You should be able to find string in all sorts of colours, so get creative and choose your own striped colour scheme. Or, work the bag in a solid colour and use a contrasting colour for the edging. Although the bag is worked in simple double crochet, you need to keep track of the increases as you work, so choose this as your third or fourth project if you are an absolute beginner.

here's how...

This String Shopper is made in three pieces; there are two side panels and a single piece for the front and back. The front and back piece is an oval shape, so the double crochet is worked in rounds instead of rows. Increases are worked at each end of the oval to create the rounded ends (see page 24 for instructions for how to work simple increases). By placing markers as explained in the pattern instructions you will be able to position the increases with ease.

how big is it?
The finished bag measures approximately 25.5cm/10in tall x 37.5cm/15in wide x 7.5cm/3in deep.

which stitches?
Double crochet (dc)

how much "yarn"?
MC = twine in main colour
  300m/330yd of dark green garden twine
A = twine in first contrasting colour
  150m/165yd of olive green garden twine
B = string in second contrasting colour
  40m/44yd of light turquoise general-purpose polypropylene string
C = string in third contrasting colour
  80m/87yd of mid blue general-purpose polypropylene string
D = string in fourth contrasting colour
  40m/44yd of mid turquoise general-purpose polypropylene string

which hooks?
8.00mm, 9.00mm, and 10.00mm (US sizes L-11, M, and N-13) crochet hooks

choosing string
 The olive and dark green shades (see above) used for the String Shopper are garden twine purchased from a big garden store. The remaining shades are general-purpose string available in DIY stores.

what tension?

7 sts and 8½ rows to 10cm/4in measured over dc using two strands MC held tog and 10.00mm (US size N-13) hook.

any extras?

Green plastic-coated garden wire, 1mm in diameter (optional)

before you start

- Make a swatch of double crochet to check your tension before beginning. If your string is finer than the one used here, you may need to use three strands instead of two to get the right tension. (See page 25 for information about checking tension.)
- The front and back of the bag are worked in a single oval-shaped piece and the stripe pattern is worked in rounds with the WS always facing. At the end of each round the colour used is fastened off, then the next round is started by joining on the new colour in the centre of one side so the joins will be positioned at the bottom of the bag. Join in the new colour in a slightly different place in each round.
- For crochet abbreviations, turn to page 127.

make the foundation chain

The bag is made in three pieces – one piece for back and front, and two side panels.

Front and back (one piece)

Using a 10.00mm (US size N-13) hook and two strands A held tog, make 13ch.

Beg stripe patt as foll:

1st rnd (WS) Using two strands A, 5dc in 2nd ch from hook, 1dc in each of next 10ch, 5dc in last ch, then cont around other side of foundation ch and

try this!

- As an alternative, you could make a luxury version of this bag with different shades of leather string.

- To make a taller bag, simply start out with more foundation chain and work the same number of rounds. Then work the side panels taller as well.

work 1dc in each of next 10ch, join with a ss in first dc. (30dc) Fasten off.

Do not turn at end of rnds, but work with WS always facing.

Cont as foll:

2nd rnd Using two strands MC, join with a ss in a dc at centre of one side of piece, 1ch, 1dc in same place as ss, *1dc in each dc until 5dc at end is reached, then lay a strand of contrasting yarn across work to mark position of next st—called *place marker*—, 1dc in first of 5dc group, 2dc in next dc, 3dc in next dc, 2dc in next dc, 1dc in next dc, place marker*; rep from * to *, 1dc in each dc to end of rnd, join with ss in first dc. (38dc)

Fasten off.

3rd rnd Using two strands B, join with a ss in a dc at centre of one side of piece, 1ch, 1dc in same place as ss, 1dc in each dc until first marker is reached, *place marker, 2dc in next dc, 1dc in each of next 2dc, 2dc in next dc, 1dc in next dc, 2dc in next dc, 1dc in each of next 2dc, 2dc in next dc (next marker now reached), place marker*, 1dc in each dc until next marker is reached; rep from * to *, 1dc in each dc to

end of rnd, join with ss in first dc. (46dc)
Fasten off.
Work next rnd without inc, but still placing markers, as foll:

4th rnd Using two strands MC, join with a ss in a dc at centre of one side, 1ch, 1dc in same place as ss, [1dc in each dc to next marker, place marker] 4 times, 1dc in each dc to end of rnd, join with ss in first dc.
Fasten off.

5th rnd Using two strands A, join with a ss in a dc at centre of one side, 1ch, 1dc in same place as ss, 1dc in each dc until first marker is reached, *place marker, [1dc in next dc, 2dc in next dc] 6 times, 1dc in next dc (next marker now reached), place marker*, 1dc in each dc until next marker is reached; rep from * to *, 1dc in each dc to end of rnd, join with ss in first dc. (58dc)
Fasten off.

6th rnd Using two strands MC, as 4th rnd.
Fasten off.

7th rnd Using two strands C, join with a ss in a dc at centre of one side, 1ch, 1dc in same place as ss, 1dc in each dc until first marker is reached, *place marker, [2dc in next dc, 1dc in each of next 2dc] 6 times, 2dc in next dc (next marker now reached), place marker*, 1dc in each dc until next marker is reached; rep from * to *, 1dc in each dc to end of rnd, join with ss in first dc. (72dc)
Fasten off.

8th rnd Using two strands MC, as 4th rnd.
Fasten off.

9th rnd Using two strands A, join with a ss in a dc at centre of one side, 1ch, 1dc in same place as ss, 1dc in each dc until first marker is reached, *place marker, [1dc in each of next 3dc, 2dc in next dc] 6 times, 1dc in each of next 2dc (next marker now reached), place marker*, 1dc in each dc until next marker is reached; rep from * to *, 1dc in each dc to end of rnd, join with ss in first dc. (84dc) Fasten off.

10th rnd Using two strands MC, as 4th rnd.
Fasten off.

11th rnd Using two strands D, as 4th rnd.
Fasten off.

12th rnd Using two strands MC, join with a ss in a dc at centre of one side, 1ch, 1dc in same place as ss, 1dc in each dc until first marker is reached, *place marker, 1dc in each of next 8dc, [2dc in next dc, 1dc in each of next 4dc] 3 times, 2dc in next dc, 1dc in each of next 8dc (next marker now reached), place marker*, 1dc in each dc until next marker is reached; rep from * to *, 1dc in each dc to end of rnd, join with ss in first dc. (92dc)
Fasten off.

13th rnd Using two strands A, as 4th rnd.
Fasten off.

14th rnd Using two strands MC, as 4th rnd.
Fasten off.

15th rnd Using two strands C, join with a ss in a dc at centre of one side, 1ch, 1dc in same place as ss, 1dc in each dc until first marker is reached, *place marker, 1dc in each of next 8dc, 2dc in next dc, 1dc in each of next 5dc, 2dc in next dc, 1dc in each of next 6dc, 2dc in next dc, 1dc in each of next 5dc, 2dc in next dc, 1dc in each of next 8dc (next marker now reached), place marker*, 1dc in each dc until next marker is reached; rep from * to *, 1dc in each dc to end of rnd, join with ss in first dc. (100dc)
Fasten off.

16th rnd Using two strands MC, as 4th rnd.
Fasten off.

Side panels (make 2 alike)
Using 10.00mm (US size N-13 hook) and two strands MC held tog, make 4ch.

1st row 1dc in 2nd ch from hook, 1dc in each of rem 2ch. Turn. (3dc)

2nd row 1ch, 1dc in each dc. Turn.
Rep last row 9 times more.
Work edging as foll:

Next rnd 1ch, 1dc in each of first 2dc, 3dc in last dc, then cont around side of piece and work 1dc in each row end, 3dc in corner foundation ch, 1dc in next foundation ch, 3dc in next foundation ch, 1dc in

each row end to last row end, 3dc in last row end, join with a ss to first dc of row.
Fasten off.

finishing touches

Fold bag in half and mark position of foldline on each side. Pin each side panel to front and back piece with WS tog and matching centre of bottom of panel with marked centre of bag.

Using 10.00mm (US size N-13) hook and two strands MC held tog, and with side panel facing, join panel to bag with ss, working each ss through a dc on both layers.

Handles (make 2 alike)

Using a 8.00mm (US size L-11) hook and one strand MC, make 18ch.

1st row 1dc in 2nd ch from hook, 1dc in each of rem 16ch. Turn. (17dc)

Change to 9.00mm (US size M) hook and cont as foll:

2nd row 1ch, 1dc in each dc. Turn. (17dc)

Join foundation-ch edge to top of last row as foll:

Joining row Holding handle with working string at right, fold it half lengthways by bringing foundation-ch edge up in back so that it is level with top of dc of previous row, then work dc through both layers, inserting hook under both loops at top of each dc of previous row and through corresponding foundation ch with each dc.

Fasten off.

Stitch each handle in place in centre of top of bag, with handle ends 10cm/4in apart and securing them to WS of dc in last rnd.

If desired, stiffen curved edge of bag by inserting green garden wire through sts of last rnd and fastening off wire ends safely and securely so they won't poke out.

crochet in the round
The single oval piece that forms the front and back of the String Shopper is created by working the crochet in rounds and using increases to produce the curves.

double-crochet bags

These wool bags were inspired by a finely crocheted bag carried by my smartly dressed 12-year-old niece Meg on sightseeing day-trips around London last year. I have done three very different versions of this simple basic shape for you to choose from. The Beaded Bag on the left has two short handles, is edged with beads, and can be crocheted in any colour you like. The Striped Bag on page 64 (and with a detail, right) has a closing tab and a short double twisted-cord shoulder strap. The V-stitch Bag on page 66 has a long shoulder strap tipped with beaded tassels.

here's how...

Once you've followed one of the bag patterns, you'll be able to adapt it to your own versions – plain, striped, or patterned. Experienced crocheters can use the patterns to make coin purses with zippers, by using a finer yarn and a smaller hook.

how big is it?
Beaded bag: The finished bag measures approximately 16cm/6^1/$_2$in wide x 21cm/8^1/$_2$in tall.
Striped bag: The finished bag measures approximately 16cm/6^1/$_2$in wide x 21cm/8^1/$_2$in tall.
V-stitch bag: The finished bag measures approximately 17cm/6^3/$_4$in wide x 21cm/8^1/$_2$in tall.

which stitches?
- Double crochet (dc)
- V-stitch pattern (V-stitch bag only)

how much yarn?
Beaded bag
Chunky wool yarn
   2 x 100g/3^1/$_2$oz balls Rowan *Polar*
   (fuchsia – shade no. 651 – or chosen colour)

or make this!

The pattern for this bag can easily be adapted for a bigger bag. Make the Beaded or Striped Bag first and you'll figure out at once how to make a bigger bag – just make more foundation chains at the start. For a big tote, however, avoid wool and use two or more strands of a cotton yarn instead, to produce a really strong bag.

Striped bag
MC = chunky wool yarn in main colour
   1 x 100g/3^1/$_2$oz ball Colinette *Point 5*
   in chosen colour
CC = chunky variegated wool yarn in contrasting colour
   1 x 100g/3^1/$_2$ozball Colinette *Point 5*
   in chosen colour

V-stitch bag
MC = chunky wool yarn in main colour
   2 x 100g/3^1/$_2$oz balls Rowan *Polar*
   (charcoal – shade no. 647 – or chosen colour)
A = chunky wool yarn in first contrasting colour
   1 x 100g/3^1/$_2$oz ball Rowan *Polar*
   (white – shade no. 645 – or chosen colour)
B = lightweight silk and cotton blend yarn in second contrasting colour
   small amount of Rowan *Summer Tweed*
   (raspberry – shade no. 528 – or chosen colour)
(*See page 124 for yarn tips*)

which hooks?
Beaded bag: 9.00mm and 12.00mm (US size M and O/P-15) crochet hooks
Striped bag: 10.00mm (US size N-13) crochet hook
V-stitch bag: 12.00mm (US size O/P-15) crochet hook
(*See page 127 for hook comparison chart*)

any extras?
- **Beaded bag:** 13 round beads, approximately 1cm/3$/$8in in diameter
- **V-stitch bag:** 8 beads, approximately 12mm/^{1}/$_2$in in diameter
- **All bags:** strong thread for sewing on straps; plus matching fabric and sewing thread for bag lining (instructions for lining bags are given on page 121)

what tension?

Beaded bag: 8 sts and 9 rows to 10cm/4in measured over dc using 12.00mm (US size O/P-15) hook.
Striped bag: 8 sts and 9 rows to 10cm/4in measured over dc using 10.00mm (US size N-13) hook.
V-stitch bag: 8 sts and 9 rows to 10cm/4in measured over V-st patt using 12.00mm (US size O/P-15) hook.

before you start

- There is no need to check your tension before beginning, as an exact bag size is not essential.
- When making the V-stitch bag, keep track of where the rounds begin and end to work the bag correctly. To do this, before starting a round, place a contrasting strand of yarn across the crochet fabric from front to back, close up against the loop on the hook and *above the working yarn*. Start to work the first st of the following round, catching the marker in position. The marker marks the start of the round and is caught under the top of the first stitch of the round.
- *For crochet abbreviations, turn to page 127.*

beaded bag

make the foundation chain

The Beaded Bag on page 60 is worked in the round in one piece, but starts with a straight foundation chain instead of a ring of chain.
Using a 12.00mm (US size O/P-15) hook and two strands of yarn held tog, make 14ch.
1st rnd (RS) Inserting hook under only one lp of each ch (see page 19), work 1dc in 2nd ch from hook, 1dc in each of rem 12ch, then cont around other side of foundation ch and inserting hook in other side of each ch, work 1dc in each of 13ch. (26dc)

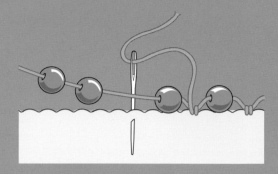

sew on the beads like this!

To sew the beads on the Beaded Bag, first thread a yarn needle with a long length of a single strand of the yarn used for the bag. Then secure the yarn to the wrong side of the top edge of the bag at a side-fold and bring it out in the middle of a "chain" at the top of a double crochet stitch. Thread the 13 beads onto the yarn. Slide the first bead up to the bag and using a separate length of yarn (the "couching" yarn), secure the beads as shown. Position each bead on top of a double crochet stitch and space the beads apart so there is one double crochet between beads. When you are finished, secure both ends of yarn to the inside of the bag.

(Do not turn at end of rnds, but keep RS always facing. Note that the side-folds of the bag will form naturally at each end of the foundation ch as the bag is worked upwards.)
Mark end of last rnd with a contrasting yarn to keep track of which side-fold is beg of rnds.
2nd rnd 1dc in each dc.
Rep last rnd until bag measures 21cm/8½in tall (approximately 19 rnds in total), ending at marked side-fold.
Work a ss in next dc and fasten off.

finishing touches

Weave in any loose ends.

Sew beads to top edge of bag as instructed in tip box on page 63.

Handles (make 2 alike)

Using 9.00mm (US size M) and two strands of yarn held tog, make 31ch.

1st row Inserting hook into back lp of each ch to make a chained edge (see page 31), work 1ss in 2nd ch from hook, 1ss in each of rem 29ch. Fasten off.

Using a strong sewing thread, sew one handle to front of bag and one to back of bag, stitching them to inside of bag and 2cm/³/₄in from side-folds.

Line bag with matching fabric (see page 121).

striped bag

make the foundation chain

The Striped Bag opposite is worked in the round in one piece, but starts with a straight foundation chain instead of a ring of chain.

Using a 10.00mm (US size N-13) hook and MC, make 14ch.

1st rnd (RS) Inserting hook through only one lp of each ch (see page 19), work 1dc in 2nd ch from hook, 1dc in each of rem 12ch, then cont around other side of foundation ch and inserting hook in other side of each ch, work 1dc in each of 13ch. (26dc)

(Do not turn at end of rnds, but keep RS always facing. Note that the side-folds of the bag will form naturally at each end of the foundation ch as the bag is worked upwards.)

Mark end of last rnd with a contrasting yarn to keep track of which side-fold is beg of rnds.

2nd rnd 1dc in each dc.

3rd rnd As 2nd rnd.

4th rnd 1dc in each dc to within last dc of rnd, 1dc in last dc breaking off MC and changing to CC with last yrh of this dc (see page 89 for instructions for how to change colours).

Cont in dc in this way, starting and stopping stripes at side-fold and working stripes as foll:

3 rnds CC.

5 rnds MC.

2 rnds CC.

4 rnds MC.

If necessary, cont in MC until bag measures 21cm/8¹/₂in tall, ending at marked side-fold.

Work a ss in next dc and fasten off.

finishing touches

Weave in any loose ends.

Closing tab

Using a 10.00mm (US size N-13) hook and MC, work a closing tab directly onto top of bag as foll:

1st row Insert hook through top of 6th dc from side-fold at top of back of bag, yrh and draw a lp through—called *join with a ss*—, 1ch, 1dc in same place as ss, 1dc in each of next 2dc. Turn. (3dc)

2nd row 1ch, 1dc in each dc. Turn.

Rep last row 5 times more.

Fasten off.

Cord holder for tab

Cut two strands MC, each 40cm/16in long. With these two strands held tog, make a twisted cord (see page 123). Knot each end of cord so knots are 7cm/2³/₄in apart. Then trim off excess yarn close to knots. To attach cord holder to front of bag, poke knots through holes in crochet below top 2 rows, positioning cord in centre of front with ends 3dc apart. Stitch knots to inside of bag.

Straps

Make two 55cm/21¹/₂in long twisted cords for straps. To make cords, cut 130cm/51in lengths of yarn, and use two strands of MC held tog to make one cord and one strand each of CC and MC held tog for other cord (see page 123).

Using strong sewing thread, stitch cord ends to inside of bag at side-folds and 1.5cm/¹/₂in below top edge.

Line bag with matching fabric (see page 121).

V-stitch bag

make the foundation chain

The V-stitch Bag opposite is worked in the round in one piece, but starts with a straight foundation chain instead of a ring of chain.

Using a 12.00mm (US size O/P-15) hook and two strands MC, make 14ch.

Using two strands MC or two strands A throughout, beg bag as foll:

1st rnd (RS) Inserting hook through only one lp of each ch (see page 19), work 1dc in 2nd ch from hook, 1dc in each of rem 12ch, then cont around other side of foundation ch and inserting hook in other side of each ch, work 1dc in each of first 12ch, 2dc in last ch. (27dc)

(Do not turn at end of rnds, but keep RS always facing. Note that the side-folds of the bag will form naturally at each end of the foundation ch as the bag is worked upwards.)

Remember to mark beg of each rnd (see Before You Start) in order to keep track of where each rnd begins and ends.

2nd rnd Using MC, 1dc in each dc. (27dc)

3rd rnd As 2nd rnd.

4th rnd *Using MC, 1dc in each of next 2dc changing to A with last yrh of 2nd dc and dropping MC at WS, insert hook from front to back through top of dc one row below next dc (in same place dc in previous row was worked), wrap A around hook and draw a lp through, drop A at WS and using MC wrap yarn around hook and draw through 2 lps on hook to complete st—called *long-dc*—*; rep from * to * 8 times more.

5th rnd Using MC, 1dc in each st.

6th rnd *Using MC, 1dc in next dc changing to A with last yrh of this st, using A work 1 long-dc in dc one row below next dc changing to MC with last yrh of this st, using MC 1dc in next dc*; rep from * to * 8 times more.

7th rnd As 5th rnd.

8th rnd Using MC, 1dc in each of first 2dc, then reposition marker to make next st first st of rnd (this is to keep beg of rnd at side-fold of bag because it moves naturally diagonally to right), *using MC, 1dc in next dc changing to A with last yrh of this st, using A work 1 long-dc in dc one row below next dc changing to MC with last yrh of this st, using MC 1dc in next dc*; rep from * to * 8 times more.

9th rnd As 5th rnd.

10th rnd Using MC, 1dc in first dc, then reposition marker to make next st first st of rnd, *using MC, 1dc in each of next 2dc changing to A with last yrh of 2nd dc, using A work 1 long-dc in dc one row below next dc changing to MC with last yrh of this st*; rep from * to * 8 times more.

11th rnd As 5th rnd.

12th rnd As 6th rnd.

13th rnd As 5th rnd.

14th rnd As 10th rnd.

15th rnd As 5th rnd.

16th rnd As 6th rnd.

Break off A.

17th rnd As 5th rnd.

18th rnd Using MC, 1dc in each dc, changing to four strands B with last yrh of last dc.

Using four strands B, work next rnd as foll:

19th rnd Using B, 1ss in back lp of each dc.

Fasten off.

finishing touches

Weave in any loose ends.

Strap

Make a double-chain cord using two strands MC for each side of cord as foll:

Using a 12.00mm (US size O/P-15) hook and two strands MC, make a slip knot, leaving 20cm/8in long loose ends. Using a separate two strands MC and again leaving long loose ends, draw a lp through slip knot to make first ch. *Using first double strand of MC, 1ch, using second double strand of MC, 1ch; rep from * alternating from one double strand of MC to the other, until strap measures 96.5cm/38in when stretched. (To make strap quicker, hold one double strand MC over forefinger in usual way, and the other over thumb.) Fasten off, leaving 20cm/8in long loose ends at end of strap.

Thread a bead onto each of four strands of yarn at each end of cord. To secure each bead, knot yarn about 4.5cm/1¾in from end of strap. Trim ends of yarn close to knots.

Using strong sewing thread, stitch strap ends to outside of bag at side-folds.

Line bag with matching fabric (see page 121).

rag handbag

Crocheting with strips of silk dupion is incredibly satisfying. The "yarn" is quick to make because the fabric tears so easily, and the lustrous colours of the silk are amazing. To form the bold double crochet stitches of this "rag" crochet bag, I used a 15.00mm (US size Q) crochet hook and two strips of the silk held together. The resulting fabric is perfect for a handbag, chunky and sturdy. If making the bag with a gusset seems a bit too advanced for your tastes, you can make two simple "rag" crochet squares for your bag, stitch them together, and add twisted-cord handles, one on each side of the bag.

here's how...

Working with silk strips creates lots of frayed ends. While you're crocheting, ignore the untidiness. Once the bag is completed you can snip off the ends.

how big is it?
The finished bag measures approximately 25.5cm/10¹/₄in tall x 31cm/12¹/₂in wide x 6.5cm/2³/₄in deep.

which stitches?
Double crochet (dc)

how much "yarn"?
A = silk fabric strips in first contrasting colour 3m/3¹/₄yd of 112cm/44in wide striped turquoise silk

B = silk fabric strips in second contrasting colour 50cm/20in of 112cm/44in wide pale turquoise dupion silk

C = silk fabric strips in third contrasting colour 90cm/1yd of 112cm/44in wide striped mid olive silk

D = silk fabric strips in fourth contrasting colour 1.4m/1³/₄yd of 112cm/44in wide light olive dupion silk

E = silk fabric strips in fifth contrasting colour 50cm/20in of 112cm/44in wide lime dupion silk

F = silk fabric strips in fifth contrasting colour 40cm/16in of 112cm/44in wide dark turquoise dupion silk

which hook?
15.00mm (US size Q) crochet hook

any extras?
- Sewing thread for joining crocheted pieces
- 40cm/16in of 112cm/44in wide dupion silk in chosen colour for lining and matching thread

what tension?
Approximately 4¹/₂ sts and 5¹/₂ rows to 10cm/4in measured over dc using two fabric strips held tog and 15.00mm (US size Q) hook.

before you start
- Cut or tear the fabric strips about 3cm/1¹/₄in wide (see pages 97 and 117 for how to prepare fabric strips).
- *For crochet abbreviations, turn to page 127.*

make the foundation chain
The bag is made in three pieces – a front, a back, and a gusset.

Front and back (both alike)
Using a 15.00mm (US size Q) hook and two strips A held tog, make 15ch.
Remembering to use two strips of each colour throughout, cont as foll:

try this!
- For a less frayed effect, crochet this bag using cotton strips for your "yarn" in the colours of your choice. Cut the strips 2.5cm/1in wide. If you're on a tight budget, use fabric remnants.

- Use a strong thread for stitching the crocheted pieces of the bag together, such as silk buttonhole thread.

1st row (WS) Using A, 1dc in 2nd ch from hook, 1dc in each of rem 13ch. Turn. (14dc)

2nd row (RS) Using A, 1ch, 1dc in each dc to end. Turn.

3rd row Using A, 1ch, 1dc in each dc to last dc, insert hook in last dc, yrh and draw a lp through, drop A, then using B, yrh and draw through 2 lps on hook to complete last dc. Turn.

Break off A.

4th row Using B, 1ch, 1dc in each dc to last dc, insert hook in last dc, yrh and draw a lp through, drop B, then using C, yrh and draw through 2 lps on hook to complete last dc. Turn.

Using two strips of each colour, cont in same way, changing to new colour with last yrh of last dc of row, **and at the same time** work in dc in stripes as foll: 1 row C, 1 row D, 1 row E, 1 row D, 1 row C, and 1 row D, changing to A with last yrh of last row.

Divide for handle

Divide for handle on next row as foll:

11th row (WS) Using A, 1ch, 1dc in each of first 5dc, fasten off, miss next 4dc, join A with a ss to next dc, 1ch, 1dc in same place as ss, 1dc in each of last 4dc. Turn.

12th row Using A, 1ch, 1dc in each of first 5dc, 4ch, 1dc in each of next 5dc, changing to F with last yrh of last dc. Turn.

13th row Using F, 1ch, 1dc in each of first 5dc, 1dc in each of next 4ch, 1dc in each of last 5dc, changing to A with last yrh of last dc. Turn.

14th row Using A, 1ch, 1dc in each dc. Fasten off.

Do not trim frayed thread ends until bag is stitched tog.

Gusset

Using a 15.00mm (US size Q) hook and two strips A, make 4ch.

Beg first half of gusset as foll:

1st row Using A, 1dc in 2nd ch from hook, 1dc in each of rem 2ch. Turn. (3dc)

2nd row Using A, 1ch, 1dc in each dc. Turn.

Rep last row until piece fits from centre of bottom of front, around corner of bag, and up to first row of B (approximately 10 rows A in total). Then cont in dc matching stripes at side of bag and changing to new colour as for bag as foll:

1 row B, 1 row C, 1 row D, 1 row E, 1 row D, 1 row C, and 1 row D.

Fasten off.

Turn gusset piece around so that foundation-ch edge is uppermost and join A with a ss to other side of first foundation ch, 1ch, 1dc in same place as ss, 1dc in each of rem 2ch.

Cont in dc working same number of rows in A as first end of gusset to first row of B.

Then rep stripe sequence from ** to **.

Fasten off.

finishing touches

Weave in any loose ends.

To line bag, use crocheted front, back, and gusset as guides for size of fabric pattern pieces. Allow for a seam allowance of 1.5cm/½in all around each lining piece. Cut lining pieces and press seam allowances to WS. Pin each lining piece to WS of corresponding crochet piece and slip stitch in place with sewing thread.

Pin back and front of bag to gusset, matching stripes along sides of bag, and placing lined sides tog. Using strong sewing thread, stitch gusset carefully in place.

Snip off any frayed ends.

If you want to try "rag" crochet, making this roomy shoulder bag is a good starting point. Three strands of chunky chenille are used together for crocheting the main part of the

bag with rag strap

bag to make a firm, dense fabric. Only the strap and gusset, which are worked in one piece, are made in "rag" crochet with strips of dupion silk. Double crochet stitches are used for all the pieces of the bag, so it is extra quick and easy to make. Pick silk colours to complement the yarn colour you've chosen, and prepare the silk strips before you start, winding them into balls.

here's how...

Before you start the Bag with Rag Strap, prepare your "rag" yarn by cutting or tearing strips approximately ³/₄in (2cm) wide. Turn to page 117 for instructions for how to tear or cut fabric strips in the usual way, or to page 97 for a super-quick cutting technique.

how big is it?
The finished bag measures approximately 32.5cm/13in wide x 26cm/10¹/₂in tall x 5cm/2in deep.

which stitches?
Double crochet (dc)

how much yarn?
MC = chunky cotton chenille in main colour
    3 x 100g/3¹/₂oz balls Rowan *Chunky Cotton Chenille* (aqua blue – shade no. 392 – or chosen colour)
A, B, and C = silk fabric strips in three contrasting colours
    70cm/³/₄yd of 112cm/44in wide silk dupion in

each of lilac-grey, lilac, and turquoise or three chosen colours
(*See page 124 for yarn tips*)

which hook?
10.00mm (US size N-13) crochet hook

any extras?
- Large button and sewing thread
- Lining fabric and matching sewing thread (optional)

what tension?
- 8 sts and 8 rows to 10cm/4in measured over dc using three strands MC held tog and 10.00mm (US size N-13) hook.
- 10 sts and 7¹/₂ rows to 10cm/4in measured over dc (stretched slightly) using A (fabric strip) and 10.00mm (US size N-13) hook.

before you start
- There is no need to check your tension before beginning, as an exact size is not essential for a bag.
- *For crochet abbreviations, turn to page 127.*

make the foundation chain
The bag is made in three pieces – a front, a back, and a strap/gusset.
Front and back (both alike)
Using a 10.00mm (US size N-13) hook and three strands MC held tog, make 27ch.
1st row 1dc in 2nd ch from hook, 1dc in each of rem 25ch. Turn. (26dc)
2nd row 1ch, 1dc in each dc to end. Turn.
Rep last row until piece measures 26cm/10¹/₂in from foundation-ch edge – total of approximately 21 rows.

try this!
- To avoid having to weave in lots of loose ends, when changing colours on the "rag" crochet strap, work your crochet stitches over the ends of the silk strips.

- While crocheting the strap/gusset you'll notice that frayed threads appear. Wait until the bag is complete to trim off these threads.

Strap/gusset

The strap also forms the gusset on the bag.
Using a 10.00mm (US size N-13) hook and A,
make 6ch.
1st row 1dc in 2nd ch from hook, 1dc in each of
rem 4ch. Turn. (5dc)
2nd row 1ch, 1dc in each dc to end. Turn.
Rep last row 3 times more, changing to B with last
yrh of last dc. Break off A.
Cont in dc and work in stripes, changing to new
colour with last yrh of last dc of old colour, as foll:
*5 rows B.
5 rows C.
5 rows A.*
Rep from * to * 7 times more.
Then work 5 rows B, 5 rows C.
Fasten off.

finishing touches

Weave in any loose ends.
Sew ends of strap/gusset tog to form a ring.
Positioning strap/gusset seam at centre of
foundation-ch edge of front of bag and with WS tog,
pin strap/gusset to front along two sides and
bottom edge. With strap/gusset facing you, using
10.00mm (US size N-13) hook and two strands MC,
and starting at top of one side edge, work dc
through edge of both layers all around edge of bag,
then cont dc along free edge of strap to beg of rnd
of dc; join with a ss in first dc.
Fasten off.
Join strap/gusset to back of bag in same way.

Button loop

Make a 11cm/4¼in long twisted cord for button.
For cord, cut two 50cm/20in lengths of MC. With
these two strands held tog, make a cord as
explained on page 123.

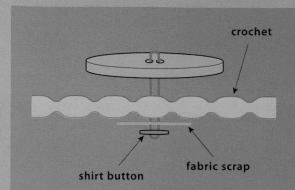

crochet

shirt button

fabric scrap

sew your buttons on securely!

Chunky, airy crochet isn't always the ideal
base for sewing on a button. When sewing the
button on this bag, I used an old tailoring
trick. By placing a scrap of matching fabric or
felt and a shirt button on the wrong side of
the crochet behind the main button you can
provide something for the sewing thread to
grab on to. Just stitch through the shirt
button, the fabric scrap, and the crochet each
time your thread catches in the main button.

Sew button to centre of front of bag 3cm/1¼in
from top edge. Attach both ends of cord to centre
top edge of back to correspond with button.
If desired, line bag with fabric (see page 121).
Trim off frayed fabric ends.

twine basket

Twine is a great choice for a sturdy shopper because it is very tough and holds its shape well. This basket starts with a circle and is worked with two strands of garden twine held together and a 12.00mm (US size O/P-15) hook. Cotton yarn and fabric strips provide the simple stripes.

The basket gave me a platform to indulge my love of beads. Searching for just the right beads for the finished piece was nearly as enjoyable as the crocheting process. In the end I chose two alternative bead types, the ones in neutral shades (see left) dress the basket down a bit and the bright yellow ones (see right and top left) give it a snappier look. Take the twine and samples of the stripe accents with you when you choose your beads to get just the right colour.

here's how...

The basket is worked round and round in a continuous spiral, so be sure to place the marker at the beginning of each round to keep track of where rounds begin and end (see the tip box opposite).

how big is it?
The finished basket measures approximately 26cm/10¼in in diameter x 30.5cm/12¼in tall.

which stitches?
Double crochet (dc)

how much "yarn"?
MC = twine in main colour
   350m/383yd of natural garden twine
A = cotton fabric strips in first contrasting colour
   20cm/¼yd of 135cm/53in wide green cotton, or
   30cm/½yd of 112cm/44in wide green cotton
B = medium-weight cotton yarn in second contrasting colour
   1 x 50g/1¾oz ball Rowan *All Seasons Cotton* (turquoise – shade no. 185 – or chosen colour)
(*See page 124 for yarn tips*)

which hook?
12mm (US size O/P-15) crochet hook

or make this!

Twine and rags are perfect candidates for a rug. To make a rug, start out as for the basket, then after the eighth round carry on increasing twelve stitches on every alternate round until the rug is the desired size.

what tension?
6 sts and 7½ rows to 10cm/4in measured over dc using two strands MC held tog and 12mm (US size O/P-15) hook.

any extras?
- 6 or 16 beads, 12mm/½in in diameter
- Sewing thread for stitching on beads

before you start
- Make a swatch of double crochet to check your tension before beginning. If your twine is finer or thicker than the one used here, you may need to use more or fewer strands to get the right tension. (See page 25 for more about tension.)
- Cut (or tear) your fabric strips 2–2.5cm/¾–1in wide (see pages 97 and 117 for how to prepare fabric strips).
- To change to a new colour, drop the colour you are working with when there are two loops on the hook and complete the dc with the new colour (see page 89).
- Work over the ends of the yarns to avoid having to weave them in later.
- *For crochet abbreviations, turn to page 127.*

make the foundation ring
Using a 12mm (US size O/P-15) hook and two strands MC held tog, make 4ch and join with a ss in first ch to form a ring.
1st rnd (RS) 1ch, 8dc in ring. (Do not turn at end of rnds, but work with RS always facing.)
Position marker as explained opposite.
2nd rnd 2dc in each dc. (16dc)
3rd rnd *1dc in next dc, 2dc in next dc; rep from * to end. (24dc)
4th rnd 1dc in each dc to end of rnd.

5th rnd *1dc in next dc, 2dc in next dc; rep from * to end. (36dc)

6th rnd As 4th rnd.

7th rnd *1dc in each of next 2dc, 2dc in next dc; rep from * to end. (48dc)

8th rnd As 4th rnd.

9th rnd As 4th rnd.

10th rnd Working into back lp of top of each dc, work 1dc in each dc to end.

(The last rnd forms a lip around base of basket, and rem rnds are worked without incs so that the basket grows upwards.)

11th rnd Working into both lps of top of each dc in usual way, 1dc in each dc to end of rnd.

12th rnd As 11th rnd.

13th rnd As 11th rnd, but dropping MC inside basket and changing to A (fabric strip) with last yrh of last dc.

14th rnd Using A, as 11th rnd, but dropping A and changing back to two strands MC with last yrh of last dc.

Break off A.

Carrying MC up WS of crochet and breaking off B and A after each stripe, cont in dc in stripes as foll:

7 rnds, using two strands MC.

1 rnd, using three strands B.

3 rnds, using two strands MC.

1 rnd, using A (fabric strip).

2 rnds, using two strands MC.

Handles

Cont with two strands MC, start handles on next rnd as foll:

Next rnd 1dc in each of first 10dc, 8ch, miss next 4dc, 1dc in each of next 20dc, 8ch, miss next 4dc, 1dc in each of last 10dc.

Next rnd 1dc in each dc and each ch to end. (56dc)

Next 2 rnds 1dc in each dc to end.

Work 1ss in next dc and fasten off.

keep track of your rounds!

To keep track of where rounds start and finish, position a strand of contrasting yarn at the end of each round. To do this, before starting the next round, place the contrasting strand across the crochet fabric from front to back, close up against the loop on the hook and above the working yarn (see coloured marker above). Start to work the first double crochet of the following round, catching the marker in position (see arrow above). The marker marks the start of the round and is caught under the top of the first stitch of the round. It is pulled out afterwards.

finishing touches

Weave in any loose ends.

Stitch 16 beads around bag, or only three beads under each handle. Sew beads in place with sewing thread, positioning them just below last stripe in A and with 3dc between them.

net bags

Net bags are super-handy. Because they scrunch up into practically nothing, you can carry one around in your handbag and pull it out as the need arises. Here are three crochet versions of this practical bag, each with a different strap. They are made in one piece with rows of double crochet, but when worked on a huge hook and stretched out for use, this simple stitch is hard to recognize. Shown here, the Bag with Leather Handles is worked with a stylish tape yarn and the handles are added at the end (see page 85 for instructions). Twisted cords form the handles for the cotton Drawstring Bag on page 83. Embroidery hoops were used on the Bag with Wooden Handles on page 84.

here's how...

These bags look small as you crochet them, but they expand to hold quite a lot. The airy, open look of the crochet fabric only appears when you stretch it before joining the side seams.

how big is it?
Drawstring bag: The finished bag measures approximately 38cm/15in wide x 30.5cm/12in tall, excluding ruffle above drawstring.
Bag with wooden handles: The finished bag measures approximately 38cm/15in wide x 30.5cm/12in tall.
Bag with leather handles: The finished bag measures approximately 38cm/15in wide x 30.5cm/12in tall.

which stitches?
Double crochet (dc)

how much yarn?
Drawstring bag
MC = medium-weight cotton yarn in main colour
2 x 50g/1³/₄oz balls Rowan *All Seasons Cotton* (coral – shade no. 183 – or chosen colour)
CC = medium-weight cotton yarn in contrasting colour
small amount of Rowan *All Seasons Cotton* (grey – shade no. 170 – or chosen colour)
Bag with wooden handles
Cotton tape yarn
3 x 50g/1³/₄oz balls Rowan *Cotton Tape* (purple – shade no. 550 – or chosen colour)
Bag with leather handles
Linen and cotton tape yarn
3 x 50g/1³/₄oz balls Rowan *Linen Tape* (shade no. 347 – or chosen colour)
(*See page 124 for yarn tips*)

which hooks?
8.00mm and 15.00mm (US sizes L-11 and Q) crochet hooks

any extras?
- **Bag with wooden handles:** two wooden embroidery hoop frames 12.5cm/5in in diameter (or wooden ring handles from a craft shop), painted with acrylics in desired colour; plus 16 beads with large eyes (eight each of two different bead types)
- **Bag with leather handles:** 10m/11yd leather string (2mm in diameter) in desired colour

what tension?
Approximately 8 sts and 8 rows to 10cm/4in measured over dc (unstretched) using 15.00mm (US size Q) hook.

before you start
- There is no need to check your tension before beginning, as an exact size is not essential for a bag.
- Working the foundation chain for the bags loosely, as instructed, makes the first row easier.
- *For crochet abbreviations, turn to page 127.*

drawstring bag

make the foundation chain
The Drawstring Bag on the opposite page is worked in one long piece that is folded in half.
Using a 15.00mm (US size Q) hook and MC, make 31ch loosely.
1st row 1dc in 2nd ch from hook, 1dc in each of rem 29ch. Turn. (30dc)

2nd row 1ch, 1dc in each dc to end. Turn.
Rep last row 36 times more (for a total of 38 rows worked from beg).
Do not fasten off MC.

finishing touches

Change to a 8.00mm (US size L-11) hook and cont with MC to work edging on next row of bag as foll:
Edging row (RS) 1ch, [1dc in next dc, 2dc in next dc] 15 times.
Fasten off.
Using a 8.00mm (US size L-11) hook and MC, work edging along other end (foundation-ch end) of bag with RS facing as foll:
Edging row (RS) Join on yarn with a ss in hole above first foundation ch (between sts of first row), 1ch, 1dc in same place as ss, 2dc in next hole above next foundation ch, [1dc in next hole, 2dc in next hole] 14 times.
Fasten off.
Seams
To elongate sts, stretch crochet lengthways before joining side seams. Then fold bag in half widthways, with WS tog and lining up holes (between rows) along sides of crochet.
Using a 8.00mm (US size L-11) hook and MC and beg at bottom of one side seam, join on yarn with a ss in first hole along edge (inserting hook through both layers), 1ch, 2dc in same place as ss, 2dc in each hole to top, working last dc through edging at top of bag. Join other side seam in same way, but starting at top of bag.
Weave in any loose ends.
Drawstring cords
See tip box right for how to make two drawstrings for the bag.

drawstring cords

The drawstrings for the Drawstring Bag are two twisted cords. Each of the cords measures 122cm/48in long including the knotted ends. To make the cords, cut two 3.7m/4yd lengths of the contrasting colour (CC) and one 3.7m/4yd length of the main colour (MC). Make twisted cords from these lengths held together as explained on page 123. Thread the drawstrings through the bag below the third row from the top of the bag, with the ends of one drawstring at one side seam and the ends of the second drawstring at the other side seam. Knot the ends of each cord together.

wooden handles

I bought two small embroidery hoops for the handles for the Bag with Wooden Handles above. These hoop frames come in a range of sizes, so, if you like, you can use bigger ones to change the look of the bag.

bag with wooden handles

make the foundation chain

The Bag with Wooden Handles shown above is worked in one piece that is folded in half.
**Using a 15.00mm (US size Q) hook, make 31ch loosely.
1st row 1dc in 2nd ch from hook, 1dc in each of rem 29ch. Turn. (30dc)
2nd row 1ch, 1dc in each dc to end. Turn.

Rep last row 34 times more (for a total of 36 rows worked from beg). Do not fasten off yarn.**

finishing touches

Change to a 8.00mm (US size L-11) hook and join crochet to first wooden hoop handle with dc as foll:
Joining row (RS) Hold hook with lp in front of wooden hoop handle and hold working yarn behind (and inside) hoop, then reach over hoop and 1ch; next, insert hook through first dc of row (below hoop), reach under hoop, yrh and draw a lp through, reach above hoop, yrh and draw through 2 lps on hook to complete dc; cont in this way working 1dc in each dc to end (work sts close tog but not too tightly so sts can still slide along hoop).
Fasten off.
Join second hoop handle to other end (foundation-ch end) of bag in same way, but starting with a ss in first foundation ch.
Seams
***To elongate sts, stretch crochet lengthways before joining side seams. Then fold bag in half widthways, with WS tog and lining up holes (between rows) along sides of crochet.
Using a 8.00mm (US size L-11) hook and beg at bottom of one side seam, join on yarn with a ss in first hole along edge (inserting hook through both layers), 1ch, 2dc in same place as ss, 2dc in each hole to within last 6 holes from handle, 1dc in 6th hole from handle.
Fasten off.
Join other side seam in same way, but starting at 6th hole from handle and working towards bottom fold.
Weave in any loose ends.***
Attach beads
String four beads onto a 30cm/12in long strand of yarn, using two beads of each bead type. To hold on beads, make a knot at each end of strand so knots are 23cm/9in apart. Trim yarn ends close to knots. With two beads at each end of knotted strand, fold strand in half and loop onto an end st on handle

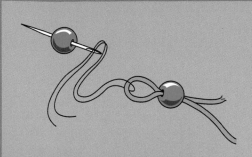

string the beads like this!

Even if your beads have big holes, it may not be that easy to pass crochet yarn through them. Here's a foolproof method. Fold a length of sewing thread in half and pass the two ends through a fine sewing needle. Then just loop the yarn through the loop of sewing thread and draw it through the beads one at a time as shown above.

(attach as you would fringe – see page122 for how to attach fringe). Make three more beaded strands and attach to three rem end sts on handles.

bag with leather handles

make the foundation chain

To work the Bag with Leather Handles on page 81, work as for Bag with Wooden Handles from ** to **.

finishing touches

Before joining last row of crochet to a handle, set aside and make handles as foll:

Leather handles

Cut a piece of cardboard 16.5cm/6½in wide. Then leaving a 13cm/5in length at beg, wrap leather string loosely five times around cardboard. Knot

short loose end to long loose end close to cardboard and slip wraps off cardboard, keeping rings tog. With long loose end and 8.00mm (US size L-11) hook, work 18dc loosely around leather rings, spacing sts apart. Do not fasten off, but set aside. Next, pick up crochet again, and using a 8.00mm (US size L-11) hook and yarn, join crochet to unworked section of leather handle with dc as foll:

Joining row (RS) Hold hook with lp in front of leather handle and hold working yarn behind (and inside) handle, then reach over handle and 1ch; next, insert hook through first dc of row (below handle), reach under handle, yrh and draw a lp through, reach above handle, yrh and draw through 2 lps on hook to complete dc; cont in this way working 1dc in each dc to end (work sts close tog but not too tightly so sts can still slide along handle).

Fasten off.

If there is still any uncovered section on handle, cover with a few more leather dc, then fasten off leather. Thread leather ends inside yarn dc on handle. Secure each end of joining row to a leather dc with a few sts using yarn and yarn needle.

Make and join on a second handle to other end (foundation-ch end) of bag in same way, but starting with a ss in first foundation ch.

Seams

Work seams as for Bag with Wooden Handles from *** to ***.

striped throw

Crochet is great for making throws from soft, cosy yarns. Unlike knitting, crochet can be worked across any width because only one stitch is worked at once. With knitting all the stitches have to fit onto a long circular needle, so there's a limit to the size of the piece. This generous-size, lightweight throw is made with chunky cotton chenille worked in treble crochet and striped with a superchunky wool worked in double crochet. Amazingly, I made it, excluding the fringing, in about 12 hours. And I'm not a particularly speedy crocheter. The fringe softens the whole effect of the texture and, as with all finishing touches, it should be added with care to give your work the treasured heirloom look.

here's how...

You can use the stripe pattern given in these instructions or create your own stripe variation. Using the same two contrasting colours for the throw, you can make any number of stripe combinations, varying the thickness of the stripes. If the colour is changed every two or four rows, there is no need to break off the yarn after every stripe – you can simply carry the yarn up the side of the throw.

how big is it?
The finished throw measures approximately 122cm/48³⁄₄in wide x 157cm/62in long.

which stitches?
- Double crochet (dc)
- Treble crochet (tr)

how much yarn?
MC = chunky cotton chenille yarn in main colour
   9 x 100g/3¹⁄₂oz balls Rowan *Chunky Cotton*

try this!

- To avoid having to weave in lots of loose ends, when changing colours lay the loose ends of yarn over the top of the previous row and work your stitches over them.

- When working the chenille stripes in this throw, use two strands of it held together to create a thicker yarn. The best way to do this is to pull one strand out of the centre of the ball and pair it with the strand starting on the outside of the ball.

   Chenille (aqua blue – shade no. 392 – or chosen colour)
CC = superthick yarn in contrasting colour
   5 x 100g/3¹⁄₂oz balls Rowan *Big Wool*
   (blue – shade no. 010 – or chosen colour)
(See page 124 for yarn tips)

which hook?
15.00mm (US size Q) crochet hook

what tension?
- 6 sts to 10cm/4in measured over stripe patt using 15.00mm (US size Q) hook.
- 5 stripe patt rows (3 rows tr using two strands MC held tog and 2 rows dc using one strand CC) to 14cm/5¹⁄₂in using 15.00mm (US size Q) hook.

before you start
- There is no need to check your tension before beginning, as an exact size is not essential for a throw.
- To create a chain edge along the foundation-chain edge of the throw, work the first row of dc into the back loop of each chain (see page 31).
- When making the throw, remember to always use two strands of the chenille yarn (MC) held together, but use only one strand of the superthick wool yarn (CC).
- *For crochet abbreviations, turn to page 127.*

make the foundation chain
Using a 15.00mm (US size Q) hook and CC, make 74ch. Beg stripe patt as foll:
1st row Using CC, 1dc in 2nd ch from hook, 1dc in each of rem 72ch. Turn. (73dc)
2nd row Using CC, 1ch, 1dc in each dc to end, changing to two strands MC with last yrh of last dc

of row (see right for how to change colours). Turn. Break off CC.

Cont patt using two strands MC and one strand CC throughout as foll:

3rd row Using MC, 3ch (to count as first tr), miss first dc, *1tr in next dc; rep from * to end. Turn. (73 sts)

4th row Using MC, 3ch, miss first tr, *1tr in next tr; rep from *, ending with 1tr in 3rd of 3ch. Turn.

5th row As 4th row, but changing to CC with last yrh of last tr of row. Turn. Break off MC.

6th row Using CC, 1ch, 1dc in each tr to end, ending with 1dc in 3rd of 3ch. Turn.

7th row Using CC, 1ch, 1dc in each dc to end, changing to MC with last yrh of last dc of row. Turn. Break off CC.

Rep 3rd–7th rows to form stripe patt and cont in stripe patt until throw measures approximately 157cm/62in long, ending with 2 CC rows. Fasten off.

finishing touches

Weave in any loose ends.

Side edging

Using a 15.00mm (US size Q) hook and CC, work a row of dc along two sides of throw from top of last row to foundation-ch edge. To work this edging, work 4dc evenly along row-ends of each MC stripe and 2dc along row-ends of each CC stripe.

Fringe

Attach 25 groups of fringe evenly along top and bottom of throw (foundation-ch edge and last-row edge). For each group of fringe, use eight strands of MC, each 40cm/16in long. Fold each group of eight strands in half and pull through edge of throw (see page 122). To attach fringe groups evenly, position

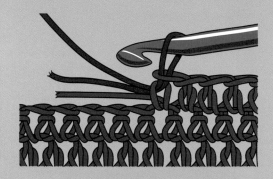

change colours like this!

When changing colours in your crochet it is usually best to do so when completing the last loop of the previous stitch. This is so that the loop on the hook after you have completed the stitch is in the new colour and will match the colour used for the next stitch. Whether changing colours at the end of a row or in the middle of the row (as shown above), complete whatever stitch you are working up to the last loop needed, then draw through the new colour to finish the stitch. The illustration above shows a completed double crochet with the new colour on the hook ready to start the next stitch. The same principle applies for half treble crochet or treble crochet.

one group in first and last st of foundation ch, and one group in every 3rd st of foundation ch in between.

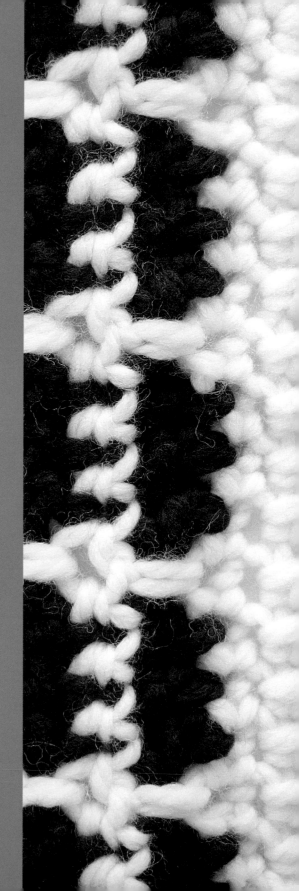

patterned throws

Made with simple pattern stitches, these two throws will give you a taste of how basic crochet stitches can be combined to make smart multicoloured textures. The Brick-stitch Throw on the left uses three colours and is edged with one row of simple treble crochet. Made with a hook 15 millimetres in diameter (US size Q) and superthick wool yarns, the giant loops have a surprisingly contemporary look. The black-and-white Bicolour Throw shown right and on page 93 is just as quick and easy – you can make it in any two colours you like. After working only a few rows of either throw, you'll be able to continue without even reading the pattern again.

here's how...

The Brick-stitch Throw shown on page 90 has written row-by-row instructions. For the row-by-row instructions for the Bicolour Throw (see detail opposite), follow the simple symbol chart provided.

how big is it?
Brick-stitch throw: The finished throw measures approximately 130cm/52in wide x 168cm/67in long.
Bicolour throw: The finished throw measures approximately 122cm/48¾in wide x 149cm/58½in long.

which stitches?
- Treble crochet (tr), for Brick-stitch Throw
- Treble crochet (tr) and double crochet (dc), for Bicolour Throw

how much yarn?
Brick-stitch throw

A = superchunky wool yarn in first contrasting colour
6 x 100g/3½oz balls Rowan *Big Wool*
(black – shade no. 008 – or chosen colour)
B = superchunky wool yarn in second contrasting colour
7 x 100g/3½oz balls Rowan *Big Wool*
(grape – shade no. 025 – or chosen colour)
C = superchunky wool yarn in third contrasting colour
6 x 100g/3½oz balls Rowan *Big Wool*
(white – shade no. 001 – or chosen colour)

Bicolour throw

MC = superchunky wool yarn in main colour
9 x 100g/3½oz balls Rowan *Big Wool*
(white – shade no. 001 – or chosen colour)
CC = superchunky wool yarn in contrasting colour
8 x 100g/3½oz balls Rowan *Big Wool*
(black – shade no. 008 – or chosen colour)
(*See page 124 for yarn tips*)

which hooks?
12.00mm and 15.00mm (US sizes O/P-15 and Q) crochet hooks

what tension?
Brick-stitch throw: Approximately 6½ sts and 5 rows to 10cm/4in measured over brick-stitch patt using 15.00mm (US size Q) hook.
Bicolour throw: 6 sts and 5 rows to 10cm/4in measured over bicolour patt using 15.00mm (US size Q) hook.

before you start
- There is no need to check your tension before beginning, as an exact size is not essential for a throw.
- *For crochet abbreviations, turn to page 127.*

brick-stitch throw

make the foundation chain
Using a 15.00mm (US size Q) hook and A, make 84ch.
1st patt row 1tr in 4th ch from hook, 1tr in each of next 3ch, 4ch, miss next 4ch, *1tr in each of next 4ch, 4ch, miss next 4ch; rep from *, ending with 1tr in last ch. Turn. (82 sts, counting each ch, each tr, and 3ch at beg of row as one st)
Drop A at side of work, but do not break off.
2nd patt row Using B, 3ch, 1tr in each of first 4ch missed in last row (working around 4ch above), 4ch, miss next 4tr, *1tr in each of next 4ch missed in last row, 4ch, miss next 4tr; rep from *, ending with 1dc in 3rd of 3ch. Turn.
Drop B at side of work, but do not break off.
3rd patt row Using C, 3ch, 1tr in each of first 4tr

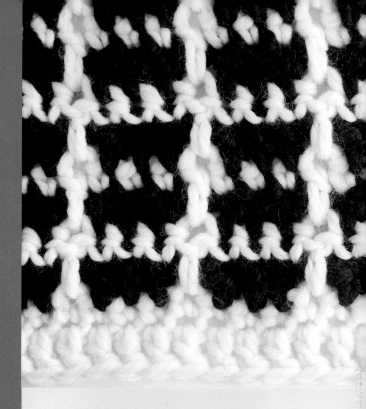

missed in last row, 4ch, miss next 4tr, *1tr in each of
next 4tr missed in last row, 4ch, miss next 4tr; rep
from *, ending with 1dc in 3rd of 3ch. Turn.
Drop C at side of work, but do not break off.
4th patt row Using A, as 3rd patt row.
Drop A at side of work, but do not break off.
5th patt row Using B, as 3rd patt row.
Drop B at side of work, but do not break off.
Rep 3rd–5th patt rows to form patt and cont in patt
until throw measures 164cm/65¹/₂in from
foundation-ch edge, ending with a 3rd patt row.
Break off B and C and work last row as foll:
Last row Using A, 2ch, 1tr in each of first 4tr missed
in last row, 1dc in each of next 4tr, *1tr in each of
next 4tr missed in last row, 1dc in each of next 4tr;
rep from *, ending with 1dc in 3rd of 3ch.
Fasten off.

finishing touches

Using a 12.00mm hook (US size O/P-15) and B, work
tr edging around throw as foll:
Edging rnd Starting along foundation-ch edge, join
B with a ss to corner ch of foundation, 3ch to count
as first tr, 2tr in same place as ss, 1tr in each ch to
last ch, 3tr in last ch; work tr evenly along side edge;
3tr in first st along top of throw, 1tr in each st to last
st, 3tr in last st; work tr evenly along second side
edge; join with a ss to 3rd of 3ch at beg of rnd.
Fasten off.
Weave in any loose ends.

bicolour throw

Using a 15.00mm (US size Q) hook and MC,
make 72ch. Foll symbol chart below (see page
17 for symbol key) for patt, using MC for first
and 3rd rows and CC for 2nd row. Work first
row (71dc), then extend loop on hook, remove
hook and return to beg of row just worked
to work 2nd row in CC (starting with a ss).
At beg of 3rd row, pull extended MC loop
through CC loop, then work 3rd row in MC.
(Work tr in 3rd row into missed dc in row
below and around ch.)
Rep 2nd and 3rd rows to form patt, until
throw measures 145cm/57in. Fasten off. Finish
as for Brick-stitch Throw, using MC for edging.

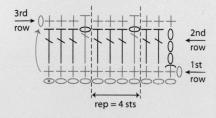

circle rag rug

The circular shape of this huge-hook rug is formed by working double crochet round and round in a spiral. The colour scheme and stripe sequence is just a suggestion. Choose five colours that harmonize nicely and that suit your décor. A bicolour rug would also be effective – perhaps with a dark solid ground and a single-row stripe on every fifth row. With the exception of fabrics that are too thick or too stiff, most materials are fine for "rag" crochet. The cotton fabrics used for the "yarn" on this rug give the crochet body, and the felt strips add a lovely contrasting texture.

here's how...

There is no need to exactly match the specified stitch size for this rug (see What Tension?). In fact, the crochet circle pattern works for any stitch size, and you can keep working the rug round and round until it is the desired size.

how big is it?
The finished rug measures approximately 36¼in/91cm in diameter, but the size is adjustable.

which stitches?
Double crochet (dc)

how much "yarn"?
A = cotton fabric strips in first contrasting colour 1.8m/2yd of 112cm/44in wide lavender cotton

B = felt strips in second contrasting colour 1.5m/1¾yd of 94cm/37in wide gold felt

C = cotton fabric strips in third contrasting colour 2.2m/2½yd of 112cm/44in wide blue cotton

D = fabric strips in fourth contrasting colour 1.8m/2yd of 112cm/44in wide gold and coral polka dot fabric

E = cotton fabric strips in fifth contrasting colour 2m/2¼yd of 112cm/44in wide turquoise cotton

which hook?
15.00mm (US size Q) crochet hook

what tension?
Approximately 5½ sts and 5½ rows to 10cm/4in measured over dc using 15.00mm (US size Q) hook.

fabrics for "rag" crochet
A range of fabric types was used for the Circles Rag Rug, including lightweight pure cotton in three shades, gold cotton felt, and a synthetic polka dot that drapes. The cotton fabrics give the rug strength and body, so be sure to include these in your design if you are making up your own. You could also wrap each strip of fabric around string as you work; this would add extra strength and extra weight, for a very durable rug.

before you start

- Cut the felt strips 12mm/^{1}/$_2$in wide or just slightly under this width (see right and page 117 for tips on cutting). The felt can be more stretchy either across the width or lengthways, so cut the strips in the direction that is less stretchy. Cut or tear the cotton-fabric strips about 2.5–4cm/1–1^1/$_2$in wide depending on the fabric thickness – wider for fine cotton and narrower for medium-weight cotton. Make a small swatch of double crochet to test the strip width if you are unsure.
- To keep track of where rounds start and finish, position a strand of contrasting yarn at the end of each round. To do this, before starting the next round, place the contrasting strand across the crochet fabric from front to back, close up against the loop on the hook and *above the working yarn*. Start to work the first dc of the following round, catching the marker in position. The marker marks the start of the round and is caught under the top of the first stitch of the round. (See page 79 for an illustration of this marking technique.)
- To change to a new colour, drop the colour you are working with when there are two loops on the hook and complete the dc with the new colour (see page 89).
- Work over the ends of the fabric strips to avoid having to weave them in later.
- *For crochet abbreviations, turn to page 127.*

make the foundation ring

Using a 15.00mm (US size Q) hook and A, make 4ch and join with a ss in first ch to form a ring.
1st rnd (RS) 1ch, 8dc in ring. (Do not turn at end of rnds, but work with RS always facing.)
Position marker as explained in Before You Start.
2nd rnd 2dc in each dc. (16dc)

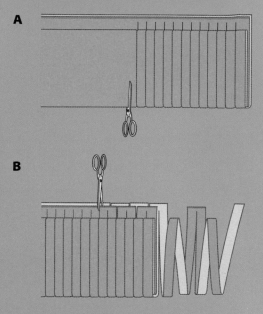

rag strips in a jiffy!

I usually tear my continuous "rag" strips for crochet, but some fabrics won't cooperate. Felt, for instance, can be torn but not in neat, even strips. If you are only cutting a few strips, you can cut back and forth as shown on page 117, but if you need to cut masses of strips, such as for a rug, try this quick technique. Fold your fabric in half lengthways, aligning the selvedges. Then fold the fabric again lengthways, positioning the first fold about 2in/5cm from the selvedges. Starting at the second fold, cut the first strip from the fold towards the selvedges, cutting through the first fold and ending the cut about 1cm/^{3}/$_8$in from the selvedges. Continue cutting strips in this way, leaving them all joined at the top (A). To create the continuous strip, clip through the bottom layer of fabric at the top of the first strip. When you unravel the first strip, you'll see where to clip through the fabric at the selvedge to create the continuous strip (B).

Changing colours as desired (see Before You Start and illustration on page 89) and using B (felt) for at least every third or fourth row throughout, cont working rnds to shape rug as foll:

3rd rnd *1dc in next dc, 2dc in next dc; rep from *. (24dc)

4th rnd 1dc in each dc.

5th rnd *1dc in next dc, 2dc in next dc; rep from *. (36dc)

6th rnd As 4th rnd.

7th rnd *1dc in each of next 2dc, 2dc in next dc; rep from *. (48dc)

8th rnd As 4th rnd.

9th rnd *1dc in each of next 3dc, 2dc in next dc; rep from *. (60dc)

10th rnd As 4th rnd.

11th rnd 1dc in each of first 2dc, 2dc in next dc, *1dc in each of next 4dc, 2dc in next dc; rep from *, ending with 1dc in each of last 2dc. (72dc)

12th rnd As 4th rnd.

13th rnd *1dc in each of next 5dc, 2dc in next dc; rep from *. (84dc)

14th rnd As 4th rnd.

15th rnd 1dc in each of first 3dc, 2dc in next dc, *1dc in each of next 6dc, 2dc in next dc; rep from *, ending with 1dc in each of last 3dc. (96dc)

16th rnd As 4th rnd.

17th rnd *1dc in each of next 7dc, 2dc in next dc; rep from *. (108dc)

18th rnd As 4th rnd.

19th rnd 1dc in each of first 4dc, 2dc in next dc, *1dc in each of next 8dc, 2dc in next dc; rep from *, ending with 1dc in each of last 4dc. (120dc)

20th rnd As 4th rnd.

21st rnd *1dc in each of next 9dc, 2dc in next dc; rep from *. (132dc)

22nd rnd As 4th rnd.

23rd rnd 1dc in each of first 5dc, 2dc in next dc, *1dc in each of next 10dc, 2dc in next dc; rep from *, ending with 1dc in each of last 5dc. (144dc)

24th rnd As 4th rnd.

25th rnd *1dc in each of next 11dc, 2dc in next dc; rep from *. (156dc)

(If desired cont in this way, adding 12 extra dc in every alternate rnd until rug is desired size.)

Work 1ss in next dc and fasten off.

finishing touches

Weave in any loose ends of fabric strips into stitches on WS of rug.

or make this!

- This circle pattern can be used for many other things, using the same "rag" fabrics. For a cushion cover, work two circles of the desired size. With wrong sides facing and using double-sided backstitch (see page 120) for an outside seam, stitch the circles together leaving an opening for inserting the cushion pad/pillow-form. Then insert the cushion pad/pillow-form and stitch the opening closed.

- You could also use the pattern to make a circular bag. Make two pieces to the size you want, then sew them together as for the cushion suggestion, and add a strap.

square medallion cushion

This variegated yarn is just sensational. Its vibrant colours and the thin and thick texture are really eyecatching. To show it off to the full, I have crocheted it into a simple square medallion shape to make a cushion. Worked from the centre outwards, the medallion is a traditional crochet square. Since it is worked in the round, you can make it to any size with no trouble at all. Two smaller pieces stitched together, with the addition of a strap, would make a great little bag.

here's how...

You can keep adding rounds to this cushion until it is the right size, so there is no need to worry about obtaining an exact stitch size – the tension is given just as a rough guide (see right).

how big is it?
The finished cushion measures 43cm/17in square.

which stitches?
Double crochet (dc)

how much yarn?
A = variegated chunky wool yarn in first contrasting colour
    1 x 100g/3¹/₂oz ball Colinette *Point 5*
    (dusty violet – shade no. 100 – or chosen colour)
B = variegated chunky wool yarn in second contrasting colour
    1 x 100g/3¹/₂oz ball Colinette *Point 5*
    (hot pink – shade no. 134 – or chosen colour)
C = variegated chunky wool yarn in third contrasting colour
    1 x 100g/3¹/₂oz ball Colinette *Point 5*
    (bright turquoise and blue – shade no. 18 – or chosen colour)
(*See page 124 for yarn tips*)

which hook?
12.00mm (US size O/P-15) crochet hook

try this!
When changing colours, work over ends of yarn to avoid having to weave in ends later.

what tension?
6 sts and 6 rows to 10cm/4in measured over dc using 12.00mm (US size O/P-15) hook.

any extras?
- A complementary dark cotton fabric and matching sewing thread for cushion cover – one piece 46cm/18in square for the front, and two pieces each 46cm/18in by 31cm/12in for the overlapping backs
- Cushion pad/pillow-form to fit

before you start
- When working the first round, wrap the tail end of the yarn clockwise around the ring and work your 12 double crochet stitches over it. Then later you can pull the tail end to tighten up the hole at the centre.
- In order not to confuse the slip stitch worked to join the rounds with a double crochet stitch, be sure to count the stitches between the corners as you are working them. Count your stitches at the end of the first few rounds just to make sure.
- *For crochet abbreviations, turn to page 127.*

make the foundation ring
The crochet is for the front of the cushion only and is stitched to the front of a fabric cushion cover. Using a 12.00mm (US size O/P-15) hook and A, 4ch and join with a ss in first ch to form a ring.
Beg stripe patt as foll:
1st rnd (RS) Using A, 1ch, 12dc in ring, join with a ss in first dc. (Do not turn at end of rnds, but work with RS always facing.)
2nd rnd Using A, 1ch, 2dc in same place as ss, [1dc in each of next 2dc, 3dc in next dc] 3 times, 1dc in each of next 2dc, 1dc in same place as first 2dc-

group of rnd were worked, join with a ss in first dc of 2dc-group. (20dc)

3rd rnd Using A, 1ch, 2dc in same place as ss, [1dc in each of next 4dc, 3dc in next dc] 3 times, 1dc in each of next 4dc, 1dc in same place as first 2dc-group of round were worked, break off A and using B join with a ss in first dc of 2dc-group. (28dc)

4th rnd Using B, 1ch, 2dc in same place as ss, [1dc in each of next 6dc, 3dc in next dc] 3 times, 1dc in each of next 6dc, 1dc in same place as first 2dc-group of rnd were worked, join with a ss in first dc of 2dc-group. (36dc)

5th rnd Using B, 1ch, 2dc in same place as ss, [1dc in each of next 8dc, 3dc in next dc] 3 times, 1dc in each of next 8dc, 1dc in same place as first 2dc-group of rnd were worked, join with a ss in first dc of 2dc-group. (44dc)

6th rnd Using B, 1ch, 2dc in same place as ss, [1dc in each of next 10dc, 3dc in next dc] 3 times, 1dc in each of next 10dc, 1dc in same place as first 2dc-group of rnd were worked, break off B and using A join with a ss in first dc of 2dc-group. (52dc)

7th rnd Using A, 1ch, 2dc in same place as ss, [1dc in each of next 12dc, 3dc in next dc] 3 times, 1dc in each of next 12dc, 1dc in same place as first 2dc-group of rnd were worked, join with a ss in first dc of 2dc-group. (60dc)

8th rnd Using A, 1ch, 2dc in same place as ss was worked, [1dc in each of next 14dc, 3dc in next dc] 3 times, 1dc in each of next 14dc, 1dc in same place as first 2dc-group of rnd were worked, join with a ss in first dc of 2dc-group. (68dc)

9th rnd Using A, 1ch, 2dc in same place as ss, [1dc in each of next 16dc, 3dc in next dc] 3 times, 1dc in each of next 16dc, 1dc in same place as first 2dc-group of rnd were worked, break off A and using C join with a ss in first dc of 2dc-group. (76dc)

10th rnd Using C, 1ch, 2dc in same place as ss, [1dc in each of next 18dc, 3dc in next dc] 3 times, 1dc in each of next 18dc, 1dc in same place as first 2dc-group of rnd were worked, join with a ss in first dc of 2dc-group. (84dc)

11th rnd Using C, 1ch, 2dc in same place as ss, [1dc in each of next 20dc, 3dc in next dc] 3 times, 1dc in each of next 20dc, 1dc in same place as first 2dc-group of round were worked, break off C and using B join with a ss in first dc of 2dc-group. (92dc)

12th rnd Using B, 1ch, 2dc in same place as ss, [1dc in each of next 22dc, 3dc in next dc] 3 times, 1dc in each of next 22dc, 1dc in same place as first 2dc-group of rnd were worked, join with a ss in first dc of 2dc-group. (100dc)

13th rnd Using B, 1ch, 2dc in same place as ss, [1dc in each of next 24dc, 3dc in next dc] 3 times, 1dc in each of next 24dc, 1dc in same place as first 2dc-group of round were worked, break off B and using A join with a ss in first dc of 2dc-group. (108dc)

14th rnd Using A, 1ch, 1ss in each dc, join with a ss in first ss of rnd. Fasten off.

finishing touches

Weave in any loose ends on WS. Pin crochet out to correct size RS down on a padded surface. Gently press on WS using a damp cloth and a warm iron. To make fabric cover, pin one back piece to each side of front and sew seams with a 1.5cm/½in seam allowance. Turn under and stitch 1.5cm/½in hems along outer edges of backs (edges that will be along opening). Then fold backs onto front with RS tog and stitch remaining seams, leaving overlapping edges open. Turn RS out and press.
Using sewing thread, stitch crochet to front of fabric cover so that edges meet seamlines and hide them. Insert cushion-pad/pillow-form.

graphic cushions

Worked with three strands of medium-weight cotton yarn held together, the simple traditional crochet stitch pattern used for these three cushions creates a chunky, durable texture. The Big Circles Cushion (in the foreground right) and the Ribbon-tie Cushion (in the background) are crocheted all in white. The decorative circles are crocheted separately and stitched on later. The Button Cushion, shown on page 2 (in the background) and page 109, is plain white with an integrated black button border at one end. The fastenings on all the cushions provide touches of bright contrasting colour.

here's how...

The stitch pattern on the cushions is formed with alternating chain spaces and double crochet. The double crochet stitches are worked into the chain spaces of the row below and the chain stitches are worked above the double crochet stitches.

how big is it?
Big circles cushion: The finished cover measures approximately 45cm/17³⁄₄in x 50cm/19³⁄₄in.
Ribbon-tie cushion: The finished cover measures approximately 35cm/13³⁄₄in x 50cm/19³⁄₄in.
Button cushion: The finished cover measures approximately 35cm/13³⁄₄in x 40cm/15³⁄₄in.

which stitches?
- Double crochet (dc)
- Chain spaces (ch sp)

how much yarn?
Big circles cushion
MC = medium-weight cotton yarn in main colour
   12 x 50g/1³⁄₄oz balls Rowan *All Seasons Cotton*
   (off-white – shade no. 178 – or chosen colour)
CC = chunky cotton chenille in contrasting colour
   small amount of Rowan *Chunky Cotton Chenille*
   (black – shade no. 367 – or chosen colour)
A = medium-weight cotton yarn
   small amount of Rowan *All Seasons Cotton*
   (coral – shade no. 183 – or chosen colour)
B = lightweight silk and cotton blend yarn
   small amount of Rowan *Summer Tweed*
   (raspberry – shade no. 528 – or chosen colour)
Ribbon-tie cushion
MC = medium-weight cotton yarn in main colour
   10 x 50g/1³⁄₄oz balls Rowan *All Seasons Cotton*
   (off-white – shade no. 178 – or chosen colour)
CC = chunky cotton chenille in contrasting colour

small amount of Rowan *Chunky Cotton Chenille* (black – shade no. 367 – or chosen colour)
Button cushion
MC = medium-weight cotton yarn in main colour
   7 x 50g/1³⁄₄oz balls Rowan *All Seasons Cotton*
   (off-white – shade no. 178 – or chosen colour)
CC = chunky cotton chenille in contrasting colour
   1 x 100g/3¹⁄₂oz ball Rowan *Chunky Cotton Chenille* (black – shade no. 367 – or chosen colour)
(*See page 124 for yarn tips*)

which hook?
10.00mm (US size N-13) crochet hook

what tension?
9 sts and 9 rows to 10cm/4in measured over patt st using three strands MC held tog and 10.00mm (US size N-13) hook.

any extras?
Big circles cushion: 45cm/17³⁄₄in square cushion pad/pillow-form
Ribbon-tie cushion: 35cm/13³⁄₄in x 45cm/17³⁄₄in cushion pad/pillow-form and 39in/99cm ribbon, 2cm/³⁄₄in wide
Button cushion: 35cm/13³⁄₄in square cushion pad/pillow-form and three buttons each 3.5cm/1³⁄₈in in diameter

before you start
- To work "into a ch sp", insert the hook through the space under the chain (not into the chain itself).
- There is no need to check your tension before beginning, as an exact size is not essential for a cushion. But wait until the cushion is complete before buying the pillow-form/cushion pad.

- The cushions are worked in the round, but you do not need to keep track of where the rounds beg and end. After the 3rd round has been completed, just work round and round until the cushion is the desired length.
- When one ball of yarn runs out, tie the strand from the new ball onto the end of the old ball. When you reach the knotted ends lay them over the top of the row below and work your stitches over them to hide them.
- For crochet abbreviations, turn to page 127.

big circles cushion

make the foundation ring

The Big Circles Cushion shown in the foreground on pages 104–105 is made in one piece.

Using a 10.00mm (US size N-13) hook and three strands MC held tog, make 81ch and join with a ss in first ch to form a ring.

Using three strands MC held tog, beg patt as foll:

1st rnd (RS) 1ch, 1dc in same place as ss, *1dc in each of rem 80ch. (Do not turn at end of rnds, but work with RS always facing.)

2nd rnd 1dc in first dc of previous rnd, *1ch, miss next dc, 1dc in next dc; rep from * to end. (81 sts, counting each dc and each 1ch as one st)

3rd rnd 1ch, *1dc in next 1-ch sp, 1ch; rep from * to end.

Rep [1dc in next 1-ch sp, 1ch] until crochet measures 49cm/19¼in from foundation-ch edge, ending in line with tail end of yarn at beg of crochet (this marks one side-fold on cushion cover).

Work last rnd as foll:

Last rnd Work 1dc in each 1-ch sp and 1dc in each dc to end, join with a ss to first dc of rnd. Fasten off.

twisted cord fastening

Make a 74cm/29in long twisted cord for closing the Big Circles Cushion. Cut two 185cm/73in lengths each of A and B. With these four strands held together, make a cord as explained on page 123. Weave the cord in and out of both layers of the cushion cover 5cm/2in from the edges, and knot at each end.

finishing touches

Turn tube of crochet WS out. Pin two layers tog along foundation-ch edge, aligning tail end of yarn with a side-fold. Using one strand MC, join seam. Weave in any loose ends, then turn RS out.

Big circle motifs (make 4 alike)

Using a 10.00mm (US size N-13) hook and one strand CC and leaving a long loose end, make 15ch and join with a ss in first ch to form a ring.

1st rnd (RS) 3ch, 35tr in ring, join with a ss in 3rd of 3ch. Fasten off, leaving a long loose end.

Distribute tr evenly around foundation ring.

Pin finished motifs, RS up, to cushion cover in desired positions. Using long loose ends, stitch in place around inner and outer edges.

Insert cushion pad/pillow form. Make a cord to close as explained above.

ribbon-tie cushion

make the foundation ring

The Ribbon-tie Cushion shown below and in the background on page 105 is made in one piece. Using a 10.00mm (US size N-13) hook and three strands MC held tog, make 63ch and join with a ss in first ch to form a ring.

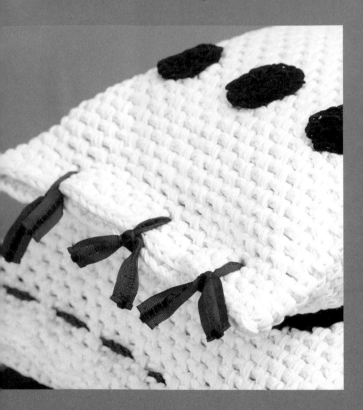

tie fastening

Adding ribbon ties is a really easy way to fasten the opening on a huge-hook crochet cushion cover. Push the ties through both layers of the crochet, about 5cm/2in from the edge, and tie or knot them together. Make sure you get a really wonderful ribbon for this important detail.

Using three strands MC held tog, beg patt as foll:

1st rnd (RS) 1ch, 1dc in same place as ss, *1dc in each of rem 62ch. (Do not turn at end of rnds, but work with RS always facing.)

2nd rnd 1dc in first dc of previous rnd, *1ch, miss next dc, 1dc in next dc; rep from * to end. (63 sts, counting each dc and each 1ch as one st)

3rd rnd 1ch, *1dc in next 1-ch sp, 1ch; rep from * to end.

Rep [1dc in next 1-ch sp, 1ch] until crochet measures 49cm/19¼in from foundation-ch edge, ending in line with tail end of yarn at beg of crochet (this marks one side-fold on cushion cover).

Work last rnd as foll:

Last rnd Work 1dc in each 1-ch sp and 1dc in each dc to end, join with a ss to first dc of rnd. Fasten off.

finishing touches

Turn tube of crochet WS out. Pin two layers tog along foundation-ch edge, aligning the tail end of yarn with a side-fold. Using one strand MC, join seam. Weave in any loose ends, then turn RS out.

Little circle motifs (make 3 alike)

Make each circle for appliqué as foll:

Using a 10.00mm (US size N-13) hook and one strand CC and leaving a long loose end, make 3ch and join with a ss to first ch to form a ring.

1st rnd (RS) 3ch, then wind loose end of yarn around back of ring once and, working over it, work 12tr in ring, join with a ss in 3rd of 3ch.

Fasten off, leaving a long loose end.

Pull loose end at centre of ring to close hole, then thread end into a yarn needle and secure with a few sts on WS.

Pin finished motifs, RS up, on cushion cover in desired positions. Using long loose end and stitching around outer edges, secure circles in place.

Ribbon ties

Cut three ribbons, each 33cm/13in long and hem the ends to desired length. Insert cushion pad/pillow-form and tie on ribbons as explained left.

button cushion

make the foundation ring

The Button Cushion shown right (and in the background on page 2) is made in one piece. Using a 10.00mm (US size N-13) hook and three strands MC held tog, make 63ch and join with a ss in first ch to form a ring.

Using three strands MC held tog, beg patt as foll:

1st rnd (RS) 1ch, 1dc in same place as ss, *1dc in each of rem 62ch. (Do not turn at end of rnds but work with RS always facing.)

2nd rnd 1dc in first dc of previous rnd, *1ch, miss next dc, 1dc in next dc; rep from * to end. (63 sts, counting each dc and each 1ch as one st)

3rd rnd 1ch, *1dc in next 1-ch sp, 1ch; rep from * to end.

Rep [1dc in next 1-ch sp, 1ch] until crochet measures 35cm/13¾in from foundation-ch edge, ending in line with tail end of yarn at beg of crochet (this marks one side-fold on cushion cover).

Break off MC. Using two strands CC, work 2 rnds more in patt, ending with 1ch. (Be sure to end in line with side-fold.)

Still using two strands CC, work buttonholes as foll:

1st buttonhole rnd 1dc in next 1-ch sp, [1ch, 1dc in next 1-ch sp] twice, [3ch, miss next 1-ch sp, 1dc in next 1-ch sp, (1ch, 1dc in next 1-ch sp) twice] 2 times, 3ch, miss next 1-ch sp, *1dc in next 1-ch sp, 1ch; rep from *, ending with 1dc in last 1-ch sp.

2nd buttonhole rnd Work in patt, but when each 3-ch sp is reached work [1dc, 1ch, 1dc] all in 3-ch sp. Work one rnd more in patt.

Work last rnd as foll:

Last rnd Work 1dc in each 1-ch sp and 1dc in each dc to end, join with a ss to first dc of rnd. Fasten off.

finishing touches

Turn tube of crochet WS out. Pin two layers tog along foundation-ch edge, aligning the tail end of yarn with a side-fold. Using one strand MC, join seam.

button fastening

There are only three buttons on the plain white Button Cushion (see page 2), so I splurged on these smart retro ones from a button store. If you have some special big buttons, base your cushion colour scheme around them.

Weave in any loose ends, then turn RS out. If buttonholes are too big for your buttons, stitch tog at each end of each buttonhole to tighten. Sew buttons in place to correspond with buttonholes. Insert cushion pad/pillow-form and button to close.

diamonds
cushion

This cushion relies on a wonderfully textured stitch and soft chenille yarn for its appeal. The simple bicolour stitch pattern forms rows of staggered diamonds and is just one of hundreds of multicoloured crochet patterns that you can find in crochet stitch pattern books. A little more complex than rows of simple double or treble crochet stitches, when used for a basic rectangular shape it is well within the reach of a beginner. Worked here with a hook 10 millimetres in diameter (US size N-13) and a thick, soft cotton chenille yarn, the cover is lined with a toning fabric.

here's how...

Using just one strand of chunky cotton chenille for this stitch pattern creates an airy, see-through texture. For a more solid texture, you could use a thicker wool yarn with the same hook size; if you do this, aim for the same tension (see right).

how big is it?
The finished cushion measures approximately 45cm/18in square.

which stitches?
- Double crochet (dc)
- Half treble crochet (htr)
- Treble crochet (tr)
- Double treble crochet (dtr)

how much yarn?
A = chunky cotton chenille yarn in first contrasting colour
  1 x 100g/3¹/₂oz ball Rowan *Chunky Cotton Chenille* (dark olive – shade no. 390 – or chosen colour)
B = chunky cotton chenille yarn in second contrasting colour
  1 x 100g/3¹/₂oz ball Rowan *Chunky Cotton Chenille* (aqua blue – shade no. 392 – or chosen colour)

try this!

A beginner should practise the stitch first – see Before You Start for how many foundation chain to start with. It is best to use a chunky wool yarn for the practice swatch because it is easier to see stitches worked in wool. Then use the chenille for the tension swatch.

C = chunky cotton chenille yarn in third contrasting colour
  small amount of Rowan *Chunky Cotton Chenille* (light sage green – shade no. 393 – or chosen colour)
(*See page 124 for yarn tips*)

which hook?
10.00mm (US size N-13) crochet hook

what tension?
7 sts and 6 rows to 10cm/4in measured over diamond patt using 10.00mm (US size N-13) hook.

any extras?
- A dark olive fabric and matching sewing thread for a fabric cushion cover – one piece 48cm/19in square for the front, and two pieces each 48cm/19in by 31cm/12in for the overlapping back pieces
- Cushion pad/pillow-form to fit

before you start
- To check tension, make 20ch and repeat 1st–6th pattern rows until sample measures 13cm/5in.
- *For crochet abbreviations, turn to page 127.*

make the foundation chain
The cushion is made in two pieces – a front and a back.
Front and back (both alike)
Using a 10.00mm (US size N-13) hook and A, make 32ch.
1st patt row 1dc in 2nd ch from hook, *1htr in next ch, 1tr in next ch, 1dtr in next ch, 1tr in next ch, 1htr in next ch, 1dc in next ch; rep from * to end, changing to B with last yrh of last dc. Turn. (31 sts) Drop A at side of work, but do not break off.

2nd patt row Using B, 3ch, miss first dc, *1tr in next st, 1htr in next st, 1ch, miss next st (dtr), 1htr in next st, 1tr in next st, 1dtr in next st; rep from * to end. Turn. (31 sts, counting first 3ch as first st)

3rd patt row Using B, 3ch, miss first dtr, *1tr in next st, 1htr in next st, 1dc in top of dtr missed in last row (working around 1ch worked in last row), 1htr in next st, 1tr in next st, 1dtr in next st, rep from *, working last dtr in 3rd of 3ch and changing to A with last yrh of this last dtr (don't pull A too tightly when picking it up from end of row 2 rows below). Turn. Drop B at side of work, but do not break off.

4th patt row Using A, 1ch, 1dc in first st, *1htr in next st, 1tr in next st, 1dtr in top of dtr 2 rows below (in same place as dc in last row), 1tr in next st, 1htr in next st, 1ch, miss next st (dtr), rep from *, omitting 1ch at end of last rep and working 1dc in 3rd of 3ch. Turn.

5th patt row Using A, 1ch, 1dc in first st, *1htr in next st, 1tr in next st, 1dtr in next st, 1tr in next st, 1htr in next st, 1dc in top of dtr missed in last row, rep from *, working last dc in dc at end of row and changing to B with last yrh of this last dc. Turn. Drop A at side of work, but do not break off.

6th patt row Using B, 3ch, miss first dc, *1tr in next st, 1htr in next st, 1ch, miss next st (dtr), 1htr in next st, 1tr in next st, 1dtr in top of dtr 2 rows below (in same place as dc in last row), rep from *, working last dtr in dc at end of row. Turn.

Rep 3rd–6th patt rows to form diamond patt and cont until 24 rows have been worked from beg (6 rows of B diamonds), ending with a 4th patt row in A. Still using A, work edging as foll:

Edging rnd Using A, 1ch, 3dc in first dc, [1dc in each of next 5 sts, 1dc in top of dtr missed in last row] 4 times, 1dc in each of next 5dc, 3dc in last dc; cont along side of piece working 29dc evenly spaced;

along foundation-ch edge work 3dc in first ch, 1dc in each ch to last ch, 3dc in last ch; work 29dc evenly along second side; join with a ss in first dc of rnd. Fasten off.

finishing touches

Weave in any loose ends on the WS.

Border

Place the crochet front on top of back, with WS tog and with dc edgings lined up. Join layers by working tr around outer edge as foll:

Using a 10.00mm (US size N-13) hook and C and working through both layers, join yarn to any corner dc with a ss, 3ch, 2tr in same place as ss, then work 1tr in each dc around three sides of cushion, working 3tr in each corner dc; along fourth side work 1tr in each dc but through one layer only to make an opening for inserting cushion pad/pillow-form; join with a ss in 3rd of 3ch.

Decorative weaving

Weave C through 2 rows as foll:

Cut three 91cm/1yd strands of C and thread onto a yarn needle. Weave yarns through sts across top row of diamonds in A, and then back across row again. Secure ends at seam. Weave C through next row of diamonds in A in same way.

Fabric cushion cover

To make fabric cover, pin one back piece to each side of front and sew seams with a 1.5cm/1/2in seam allowance. Turn under and stitch 1.5cm/1/2in hems along outer edges of backs (edges that will be along opening). Then fold backs onto front with RS tog and stitch rem seams, leaving overlapping edges open. Turn RS out and press.

Insert cushion pad/pillow-form in fabric cover, then put this inside crochet cover. Sew opening closed with invisible stitches.

yarn-and-rag cushion

Mohair yarn and dupion silk are two of my favourite materials for crochet. When crocheting swatches to test my colour scheme, I noticed how attractive the stray strands of fabric and yarn at the edge of the crochet were. Instead of trying to hide these, I decided to make them the star attraction of the design by tying them in knots to form a tasselled edging. Using this simple stitch pattern of alternating chain spaces and double crochet produces a much softer effect than double crochet does when worked on its own.

here's how...

If preferred, you can make the cushion without the self-fringe. To do this, work the first two rows of the front as for the back, then work in stripes as directed, but changing to the new colour with the last loop of the previous row (see page 89).

how big is it?
The finished cushion measures approximately 42.5cm/17in square.

which stitches?
- Double crochet (dc)
- Chain spaces (ch sp)

how much yarn?
MC = medium-weight mohair yarn in main colour
   9 x 50g/1³⁄₄oz balls Rowan *Kid Classic*
   (light blue – shade no. 818 – or chosen colour)
A = silk fabric strips in first contrasting colour
   30cm/¹⁄₃yd of 112cm/44in wide coral
   dupion silk
B = medium-weight mohair yarn in second contrasting colour
   1 x 50g/1³⁄₄oz ball Rowan *Kid Classic*
   (pink – shade no. 819 – or chosen colour)
C = silk fabric strips in third contrasting colour
   30cm/¹⁄₃yd of 112cm/44in wide mid blue
   dupion silk

try this!
If your white pillow-form/cushion pad shows through your crochet, cover it with a cotton fabric that matches the main yarn.

D = medium-weight mohair yarn in fourth contrasting colour
   1 x 50g/1³⁄₄oz ball Rowan *Kid Classic*
   (orange – shade no. 827 – or chosen colour)
E = silk fabric strips in fifth contrasting colour
   30cm/¹⁄₃yd of 112cm/44in wide terracotta
   dupion silk
(*See page 124 for yarn tips*)

which hook?
12.00mm (US size O/P-15) crochet hook

what tension?
8¹⁄₂ sts and 9 rows to 10cm/4in measured over patt st using four strands MC held tog and 12.00mm (US size O/P-15) hook.

any extras?
Cushion pad/pillow-form to fit

before you start
- This pattern is formed with chain spaces (ch sp) and double crochet. The chain space is formed by working a chain and leaving the stitch under it unworked. When working into a "ch sp", insert the hook through the space under the chain (not into the chain itself).
- Cut (or tear) your silk rag strips 2cm/³⁄₄in wide (see opposite and page 97).
- *For crochet abbreviations, turn to page 127.*

make the foundation chain
The cushion is made in three pieces – a front with stripes and two plain overlapping back pieces.
Front
Using a 12.00mm (US size O/P-15) hook and four strands MC, make 36ch and fasten off, leaving 7in/

17.5cm long loose ends at each end of foundation ch. Using a separate length of each colour for each row and leaving 17.5cm/7in loose ends at each end of each row, beg patt as foll:

1st row Using four strands MC, join MC with a ss to first ch, 1ch, 1dc in same place as ss, *1ch, miss next ch, 1dc in next ch; rep from * to last ch, 1dc in last ch. Turn. (36 sts, counting each dc and each 1ch as one st) Fasten off.

2nd row Using four strands MC, join MC with a ss to first dc, 1ch, 1dc in same place as ss, *1ch, 1dc in next 1-ch sp; rep from * to last dc, 1dc in last dc. Turn. Fasten off.

Rep last row to form patt (fastening off after each row and using four strands of MC, B, and D), **and at the same time** work in stripes as foll:

4 rows more MC, **1 row A, 1 row B, 1 row C, 1 row D, 1 row E, and 6 rows MC.**

Rep from ** to ** twice more. Fasten off.

Backs (make 2 alike)

Using a 12.00mm (US size O/P-15) hook and four strands MC, make 37ch.

1st row 1dc in 2nd ch from hook, *1ch, miss next ch, 1dc in next ch; rep from * to last ch, 1dc in last ch. Turn. (36 sts, counting each dc and each 1ch as one st)

2nd row 1ch, 1dc in first dc, *1ch, 1dc in next 1-ch sp; rep from * to last dc, 1dc in last dc. Turn.

Rep last row to form patt, working until back measures 27cm/10³⁄₄in from foundation-ch edge (approximately 24 rows).

Work last row as foll:

Last row 1ch, 1dc in each of first 2dc, *1dc in next 1-ch sp, 1dc in next dc; rep from * to end. Fasten off.

finishing touches

Knot loose ends on front tog in groups to form groups of fringe along sides as foll:

make your own yarn!

If your fabric tears easily, the quickest way to prepare the crochet strips is to tear them. When crocheted up, they look just as good as cut strips. To make a continuous strip of "rag" yarn, first straighten the end of your length of fabric. Then start at the selvedge and tear or cut a strip to the required width, stopping near the selvedge. It is generally best to stop at a distance from the edge of the fabric that is at least half the width of the strip. Turn and tear or cut in the opposite direction, stopping near the edge as before. Tear or cut back and forth in this way.

First knot ends in MC tog at each end of each MC stripe, positioning knot close to crochet. Then knot ends in A, B, C, D, and E tog at each end of rem stripes (see pages 114–115).

Lay front RS up on a flat surface and fold fringe groups onto RS. Then lay backs on top of front with RS facing, overlapping them at centre to form an envelope opening. Pin in place. Using two strands MC, overcast stitch backs to front all around outside edge (see page 120 for how to work overcast stitch). Turn RS and trim fringe groups 7cm/2³⁄₄in from each knot. Insert cushion pad/pillow-form.

useful
things to
know

seams and linings...

seams for huge-hook crochet

For a good finish, stitching seams on huge-hook crochet needs to be done quite carefully. Any flaws in seams are more obvious than on smaller-scale crocheted textures. The best method to use is a simple overcast stitch. For seams that show on the outside, double-sided backstitch makes a neat finishing touch. A cushion made from two circular pieces would be a good candidate for a decorative outside seam (see the tip box on page 98). Pieces of "rag" crochet should be stitched together either with a shallow overcast stitch, or edge-to-edge with a slip stitch, using a sewing needle and a strong sewing thread.

To weave in loose ends on huge-hook crochet, use a blunt-ended needle or a fine crochet hook to weave invisibly into the stitches. Split really thick yarns into two strands and weave in each strand separately. Clip off the woven-in ends close to the crochet. If the crochet has a wrong side that will not show, such as inside a cushion cover, you can knot together the loose ends, instead of weaving them in, and clip off close to the knot.

Working an overcast seam

Work the overcast stitches close to the edge of the two pieces of crochet. Use a blunt-ended yarn needle and matching yarn if the piece has been crocheted with yarn, and a sewing needle and thread if it has been worked with fabric strips. Place the two pieces with right sides together and edges aligned. Pin if necessary. Take a couple of stitches in the same place to start, then work stitches at equal intervals, as shown top right. Secure with a couple of stitches.

Working a double-sided backstitch seam

The double-sided backstitch looks like backstitch on both the front and the back of the work, so it is perfect for decorative, outside seams. Every other stitch on each side of the seam is double, but this will not be obvious on the finished seam since the second stitch completely covers the first stitch, matching it exactly.

Make the first stitch on the underside and work a stitch backwards on the other side of the crochet to match it, then make a stitch over the first stitch as shown by the arrow (A). Continue working the stitches as shown below, following the illustrations (B and C). Repeat steps A, B, and C along the seam (working two stitches forwards, then one stitch backwards).

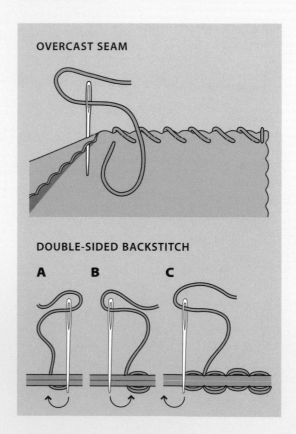

OVERCAST SEAM

DOUBLE-SIDED BACKSTITCH

A   B   C

linings for huge-hook crochet

Bags and totes that get a lot of use are best strengthened with a fabric lining. Cushion covers crocheted with huge hooks are also best lined, since the white cushion pad/pillow-form inside can show through the large textures. These linings are simply slipped on over the bare cushion pad/pillow-form before the crochet cover is put on.

If the lining fabric shows through the crochet, make sure that the colour of the lining matches the main yarn used. If the lining won't show through – for instance, inside a closely crocheted bag or tote – you can choose a complementary colour or print.

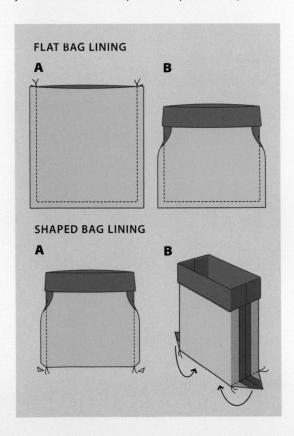

FLAT BAG LINING

A   B

SHAPED BAG LINING

A   B

Lining a simple flat bag

A bag made of two squares or rectangles is really easy to line (see Double-crochet Bags on page 60). Use the crocheted front of your bag to calculate the size of the two bag lining pieces. Add extra to the base and both sides for the 1.5cm/$\frac{1}{2}$in seam allowances and about 4cm/1$\frac{1}{2}$in at the top for a hem.

Cut two pieces of fabric to the correct size and place them with right sides together. Stitch 1.5cm/$\frac{1}{2}$in from the edge around the two sides and bottom, leaving the top open (A). Press the top of the side seams open, then fold down the top hem and press (B). Insert the lining in the bag and stitch it invisibly to the bag along the hem fold.

Lining a shaped bag

Lining a three-dimensional bag, such as the Bag with Rag Strap on page 72, is a little more difficult, but the principle is the same. Use the finished bag as the guide for cutting the lining. Measure the bag from the top edge, around the bottom, and to the top on the other side. Then measure it around the width of the bag. Allowing for 1.5cm/$\frac{1}{2}$in seam allowances at the sides and for 4cm/1$\frac{1}{2}$in hems at the top, cut the lining as one piece. If desired you can press an iron-on interfacing onto the fabric pieces before stitching them together to give the lining body.

Fold the lining in half widthways, stitch the side seams, turn down the top hem, clip off the corners at the bottom (A). Then press the seams open, pinch together a triangle shape at the two bottom corners and stitch across them as shown (B). Fold the triangle points to the underside of the bag shape as shown by the arrows to make a simple box shape. Insert the prepared lining into the bag and stitch to the inside of the bag along the hem fold.

trims for huge-hook crochet...

decorative finishes

Huge-hook crochet looks great with added
decorative trims, handmade or readymade. There
are countless pretty finishing touches available
these days – tassels, fringe, ribbons, pompoms,
braids, beads, and sequins. All you need to do is
stitch them to your finished crocheted project. You
might even want to design the crochet to suit the
trim, rather than the other way around. It's a good
way to use up delectable trims that you have
collected, but don't know what to do with.
The pompoms, beads, tassels, and fringes I've used
on my designs are just examples of how you can
decorate and personalize your own crochet.

Making your own trims is more satisfying than
buying them. If you're new to crochet, you may not
know how to make the three simple popular trims
that avid crocheters often use – pompoms
(instructions for how to make pompoms are given
on page 53), tassels, and fringes. You can make
fringes and tassels from any yarn you like, a mixture
of yarns, or even ribbon, strung beads, or fabric strips.

Although your huge-hook crochet is done in a
flash, take your time with handmade trims. Never
rush finishing touches. Perfect, carefully finished
trims will add that extra professional touch that
makes your crochet a real eyecatcher.

Making a tassel

To make a tassel, first cut lots of strands of yarn, a
little longer than twice the desired length of the
tassel. Hold the strands together and tie a separate
length of yarn tightly around the centre (A). (Leave
the ends of the tying yarn long to use for fastening
to your crochet.) Fold the tassel strands in half at the
tie and wrap another length of yarn around them to
form a "ball" of strands at the top and secure (B).

Making a fringe

To make a fringe, first cut a length of yarn at least
2.5cm/1in longer than the desired length of the
finished fringe and fold it in half. (For a plumper
fringe, use two or more strands together.) Insert a
crochet hook from back to front through the edge
of the crochet and draw the yarn through. Then
draw the ends of the yarn through the loop (A) and
pull to tighten. Work the fringe as close together
or far apart as desired (B). When the fringe is
complete, trim the ends to even them.

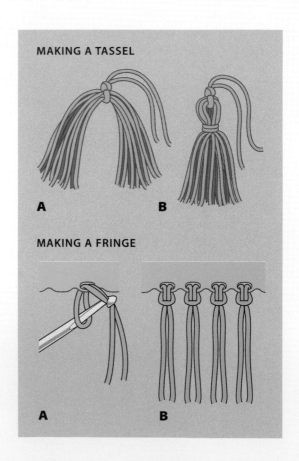

MAKING A TASSEL

A   B

MAKING A FRINGE

A   B

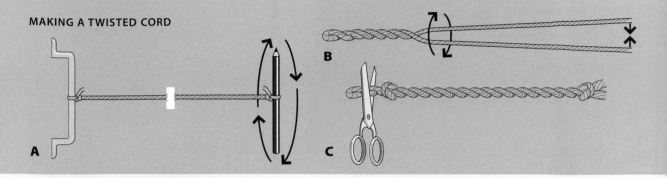

MAKING A TWISTED CORD

A

B

C

decorative fastenings and straps

The fastenings you use on bags and cushions, and the straps and handles for bags, are important finishing touches that can turn them into something really special. When creating your own huge-hook projects, focus a lot of attention on the style of the items you pick for these. Fastenings for bags can be buttons, buckles, or drawstrings; for cushions: buttons and cord ties. Avoid zippers to keep the techniques as simple as possible.

As for the straps and handles on my bag designs, there are wooden handles, crocheted leather and yarn ones, and twisted cords. Hopefully, you'll think of even more decorative fastenings, straps, and handles for your own designs. Search craft stores and fabric stores for enticing readymade cords, ribbons, and braids.

Ever wondered how you could use those delectable, unique huge buttons found in flea markets? They are ideal for huge-hook handbags and totes, and cushions. Often on huge-hook textures there's no need for buttonholes either – the buttons will pass right through the crochet.

Twisted cords feature a lot in my designs, so there are instructions for how to make them yourself on this page. A single yarn or a mixture of yarns can be used to make them. Or you can introduce a fabric strip or thin ribbon for an unusual effect. For clarity, only a single strand is shown in the instructions, but for thick cords you will need to start out with at least two strands. There is no hard and fast rule about how long to cut the strands for a specific length of twisted cord, as it depends on how stretchy the yarn is and on how tightly the cord is twisted. You will, however, need strands that are at least twice the length of the finished cord since they are folded in half to form the twist. For the twisted cords used for the projects in this book, I have indicated how many strands of yarn to use and how long to cut them.

Making a twisted cord

Cut the number of strands required, to the length specified. Then tie one end of the group of strands to a fixed object – I use a door handle. Tie the other end to a pencil. Hold the yarn loosely in one hand at the pencil end and with the other hand turn the pencil round and round (A). Keep the yarn taut as you twist it. Once the yarn starts to kink, fold it in half, still keeping it taut. Let one half of the yarn twist around the other half, releasing it gradually (B). Cut the ends of the yarn from the door handle and pencil and knot them together. Tie a knot at the folded end as well and trim off the ends (C).

buying yarn...

Yarn manufacturers change their yarn colours quite often, so it is almost impossible to guarantee that all the shades in the book will still be available when you use this book. The shade numbers used are given in the instructions if you want to use them, but feel free to use your own choice of colours.

When possible, try to buy the specific brand and type of yarn recommended in the pattern (see page 126 for addresses). However, if you need to use a substitute, be sure to buy yarn by figuring out how many metres/yards you need rather than how much in weight.

The Rowan and Colinette yarns used in this book are listed here to help you find a comparable substitute. The life-size photos of the yarns will help you find a yarn of a similar thickness. The knitting tension and needle size given for each yarn can also be used to identify yarn thickness.

Rowan yarns used in this book

All Seasons Cotton
- A medium-weight cotton yarn; 60% cotton and 40% acrylic/microfibre
- 50g/1³/₄oz (approximately 90m/98yd) per ball
- Recommended tension: 16–18 sts and 23–25 rows to 10cm/4in over st st using 4¹/₂–5¹/₂mm (US size 7–9) knitting needles

Biggy Print
- A superchunky wool yarn; 100% merino wool
- 100g/3¹/₂oz (approximately 30m/33yd) per ball
- Recommended tension: 5¹/₂ sts and 7 rows to 10cm/4in over st st using 20mm (US size 35) knitting needles

Big Wool
- A superchunky wool yarn; 100% merino wool
- 100g/3¹/₂oz (approximately 80m/87yd) per ball
- Recommended tension: 7¹/₂–8 sts and 10–12 rows to 10cm/4in over st st using 12mm or 15mm (US size 17 or 19) knitting needles

Chunky Cotton Chenille
- A chunky cotton chenille yarn; 100% cotton
- 100g/3¹/₂oz (approximately 140m/153yd) per ball
- Recommended tension: 16–18 sts and 21–25 rows to 10cm/4in over st st using 4¹/₂–5mm (US size 7–8) knitting needles

Cotton Tape
- A tubular tape yarn; 100% cotton
- 50g/1³/₄oz (approximately 65m/71yd) per ball
- Recommended tension: 13–14 sts and 17–19 rows to 10cm/4in over st st using 8mm (US size 11) knitting needles

Kid Classic
- A medium-weight mohair yarn; 70% lambswool, 26% kid mohair, and 4% nylon
- 50g/1³/₄oz (approximately 140m/153yd) per ball
- Recommended tension: 18–19 sts and 23–25 rows to 10cm/4in over st st using 5–5¹/₂mm (US size 8–9) knitting needles

Kid Silk Haze
- A fine mohair yarn; 70% super kid mohair and 30% silk
- 25g/1oz (approximately 210m/229yd) per ball
- Recommended tension: 18–25 sts and 23–34 rows to 10cm/4in over st st using 3¹/₄–5mm (US size 3–8) knitting needles

Linen Print

- A tubular tape yarn; 70% viscose and 30% linen
- 50g/1³/₄oz (approximately 55m/60yd) per ball
- Recommended tension: 13 sts and 16 rows to 10cm/4in over st st using 8mm (US size 11) knitting needles

Polar

- A chunky wool yarn; 60% pure new wool, 30% alpaca, and 10% acrylic
- 100g/3¹/₂oz (approximately 100m/109yd) per ball
- Recommended tension: 12 sts and 16 rows to 10cm/4in over st st using 8mm (US size 11) knitting needles

Summer Tweed

- A lightweight silk and cotton blend yarn; 70% silk and 30% cotton
- 50g/1³/₄oz (approximately 108m/118yd) per hank
- Recommended tension: 16 sts and 23 rows to 10cm/4in over st st using 5mm (US size 8) knitting needles

Colinette yarns used in this book

Point 5

- A chunky yarn; 100% pure wool
- 100g/3¹/₂oz (approximately 50m/54yd) per hank
- Recommended tension: 7¹/₂ sts and 9 rows to 10cm/4in over st st using 12mm (US size 17) knitting needles

Rowan *All Seasons Cotton*

Rowan *Biggy Print*

Rowan *Big Wool*

Rowan *Chunky Cotton Chenille*

Rowan *Cotton Tape*

Rowan *Kid Classic*

Rowan *Kid Silk Haze*

Rowan *Linen Print*

Rowan *Polar*

Rowan *Summer Tweed*

Colinette *Point 5*

addresses...

addresses for buying yarns

To find out where to buy Rowan or Colinette yarns near you, contact their websites:

www.knitrowan.com

www.colinette.com

For the Lion Brand novelty tape yarn shown on page 14, contact the Lion Brand website listed under Addresses for Huge Hooks (see right).

addresses for huge hooks

Try Lion Brand if, like me, you can't bear using drab grey hooks – they have a nice range of big hooks in bright colours. Alternatively, contact Needles! (in North Carolina), where you'll find a massive range of interesting hooks.

Lion Brand website: www.lionbrandyarn.com

Needles! website: jklneedles.com

about the author...

Sally Harding got hooked on crochet and knitting at the age of ten when her grandmother in Illinois taught her to do both – she went straight home and started creating outfits for her dolls. This early foray into needlework led to a lasting passion for antique textiles and embroideries, and a long line of needlework-related professions – including embroidery, crochet knitting and design; textile restoration; and craft publishing.

Sally co-authored a major needlework encyclopedia in the late 1970s and has authored and edited books and articles on crochet, knitting, and embroidery ever since. Her first crochet title was *Crochet Style*. She was the Technical Knitting Editor for *Vogue Knitting* from 1982 to 1983 when it made a comeback as the premier American knitting magazine. For many years she has edited most of the much-admired books of designer Kaffe Fassett and been endlessly inspired by his invaluable contribution to knitting.

author's acknowledgments...

First of all, I'd like to thank the team who put this book together. Thanks to John Heseltine for his stunning photographs, to Anne Wilson for her wonderful book design, and to Kate Simunek for all the fantastic illustrations. Many thanks also to Anna Sanderson and Auberon Hedgecoe at Mitchell Beazley for making this project possible and helping it to run so smoothly, and to Kate Buller and Ann Hinchcliffe at Rowan for getting me the Rowan yarns I needed so swiftly.

Thanks to my friend Nancy Thomas at Lion Brand Yarns for supplying me with coloured crochet hooks at a moment's notice and for loving knitting and crochet as much as I do.

My gratitude goes most of all to Susan Berry for her expertise on every aspect of the book process, including art direction of my crochet design, and for making me believe I could author this book.

crochet abbreviations...

To make crochet instructions easier to follow, they are written with the use of abbreviations. The abbreviations used are very logical and quick to learn, and the ones used in this book are as follows:

alt	alternate
beg	begin(ning)
ch	chain(s)
ch sp	chain space
CC	contrasting colour
cm	centimetre(s)
cont	continu(e)(ing)
dc	double crochet
dec	decreas(e)(ing)
dtr	double treble
foll	follow(s)(ing)
g	gram(s)
htr	half treble crochet
inc	increas(e)(ing)
lp(s)	loop(s)
m	metre(s)
MC	main colour
mm	millimetre(s)
oz	ounces
patt	pattern
qtr	quadruple treble
rem	remain(s)(ing)
rep	repeat(s)(ing)
rnd(s)	round(s)
RS	right side
ss	slip stitch(es)
sp	space(s)
st(s)	stitch(es)
tog	together
tr	treble crochet
trtr	triple treble
WS	wrong side
yd	yard(s)
yrh	yarn round hook

* Repeat instructions after asterisk or between asterisks as many times as instructed.

[ ] ( ) Repeat instructions inside square brackets or parentheses as many times as instructed.

English-language terminology

The names for the basic crochet stitches are different in the UK and US, which can be confusing if you pick up a crochet book when abroad. This book is written with UK crochet terminology throughout. If you are an American crocheter, be sure to follow the patterns with the following in mind!

UK	US
slip stitch (ss)	slip stitch (sl st)
double crochet (dc)	single crochet (sc)
half treble crochet (htr)	half double crochet (hdc)
treble crochet (tr)	double crochet (dc)
double treble (dtr)	treble crochet (tr)
triple treble (trtr)	double treble (dtr)
quadruple treble (qtr)	triple treble (trtr)
quintuple treble (quintr)	quadruple treble (qtr)
yarn round hook (yrh)	yarn over hook (yo)
miss (stitches)	skip (stitches)

crochet hook conversion chart

This chart shows you how the different crochet hook size systems compare, though the numbering and lettering sizes can vary from manufacturer to manufacturer. Since metric sizes are based on the diameter of the hook and tend to be more exact than the numbering or lettering size, it is best to follow these.

EU Metric	US sizes	EU Metric	US sizes
.60mm	14 steel	4.00mm	G-6
.75mm	12 steel	4.50mm	7
1.00mm	11 steel	5.00mm	H-8
1.25mm	7 steel	5.50mm	I-9
1.50mm	6 steel	6.00mm	J-10
1.75mm	5 steel	6.50mm	K-10$\frac{1}{2}$
2.00mm		7.00mm	
	B-1 (2.25mm)	8.00mm	L-11
2.50mm		9.00mm	M
	C-2 (2.75mm)	10.00mm	N-13
3.00mm		12.00mm	O/P-15
	D-3 (3.25mm)	15.00mm	Q
3.50mm	E-4	20.00mm	S
	F-5 (3.75mm)		

index...